THE EXEMPLARY LIFE OF
SAINT GERARD MAJELLA

THE EXEMPLARY LIFE OF SAINT GERARD MAJELLA

FR. O.R. VASSALL-PHILIPS, C.SS.R

PUBLISHED BY STABAT MATER PRESS

STABATMATERPRESS.COM

Cover art and interior typesetting by Stabat Mater Press. All artwork not cited is in the public domain.

ISBN (Paperback): 979-8-9997560-9-1

IMPRIMATUR
Father Edmund Surmont,
Vicar General, Archdiocese of Westminster, England,
16 September 1909

To the Most Sacred Heart of Jesus

CONTENTS

INTRODUCTION

There was a mortal, who is now above
>   In the mid glory: he, when near to die,
>   Was given Communion with the Crucified,
>   Such, that the Master's very wounds were
stamp' d
>   Upon his flesh; and from the agony
>   Which thrill'd through body and soul in that
embrace,
>   Learn that the flame of Everlasting Love
>   Doth burn ere it transform. . . .

— ST. J.H. NEWMAN, *"DREAM OF
GERONTIUS"*

SAINT GERARD MAJELLA has often been called the Thaumaturgus or Wonder-worker of the eighteenth century. Almighty God seems to have raised up this lowly Lay-brother to confute in the very age of Voltaire the flippant scepticism of a false philosophy by the stern logic of incontestable facts. It should not therefore surprise us to find his life full of marvels of all kinds.

It is, however, the duty of the author, in obedi-

ence to the decrees of Pope Urban VIII, to protest
at the outset that he attaches a purely human value
to any miracles, revelations, prophecies or other
apparently supernatural occurrences which he re-
lates in the course of this little book. That is, they
depend for their credibility – like every other al-
leged historical fact (save only those to which the
veracity of the Inspired Writers is pledged) – solely
on the testimony of men. Together with that testimony the statements based upon it will either stand
or fall.

For the well-instructed Catholic this will be a
superfluous declaration. But, as Saint Gerard's Life
may perchance fall into the hands of some who are
alien to the Catholic Faith, it may be well to state
explicitly that no child of the Church is required to
believe in the reality of any miraculous event excepting in that of those which are contained in the
Holy Scriptures. They alone rest on a Divine foundation, since of their truth we are assured not by
the fallible word or opinion of man, but by the infallible Word of God. Any other seemingly supernatural facts rest for their verification entirely on
the value of the evidence which may be adducible
in their support. If the evidence seems worthless,
we are quite free to deny the facts.

No Catholic may say that miracles have ceased.
That would be to contradict the Promises of
Christ, and to go against the clear Mind of the
Church. But with regard to any particular marvels,
we are encouraged by the proverbial caution of
Ecclesiastical Authority to shrink from arriving at
hasty conclusions, and are always permitted to use
our own judgment, provided that we do so in the
spirit of due humility and reverence, not in that of

a proud and shallow self-sufficiency which would ignorantly reject everything that lies outside the narrow bounds of its own limited experience.

With reference to the testimony on which we receive the supernatural Life of Saint Gerard, those who may desire to test its worth may be referred with confidence to the Processes of his Beatification. The author desires to state that he is himself satisfied as to the truth of all that he has related; moreover, he fails to see how anyone can arrive at a different conclusion after a careful study of the evidence, unless, indeed, he has unhappily raised a cloud of prejudice in his own mind by denying on a priori grounds the possibility of the miraculous in the abstract, notwithstanding all testimony – however overwhelming – whether human or Divine, that may be brought forward to the opposite in the concrete.

Such a man, little as he may be prepared to admit it, has in truth effectually closed the gates to any reasonable discussion; he has travelled beyond the domain where argument may hope to reach him; bowing down complacently before a wooden fetish of his own creation – a true bigot – he takes refuge behind the bulwark of generalizations that must be upheld at all costs; in the superstitious homage that he pays to the Law of Uniformity in Nature, he denies the power – sometimes even the existence – of the Supreme Lawgiver, Who most certainly can, for His own wise purposes, derogate from the order which He has Himself established.

Faith and Reason ever go hand in hand. The Catholic System harmonizes with all ascertained facts. The various forms of Rationalism, on the contrary – often mutually destructive though they are – always agree in this, that they depend for their existence on purely destructive criticism, and on theories stated with much pretence and show of learning, but which admit of no verification whatsoever. If they who prefer Faith, Reason, and Fact to impossible hypotheses and sophistical theories are, on this account, called hard names – fanatical, credulous, narrow-minded, retrogressive, Priest-ridden, and the like – it is always a consolation to remember that hard names are the one resource which yet remains to a discredited cause that has no other weapons left in its armoury.

The author also feels – to borrow the words of the late Cardinal Dechamps – that "when the miraculous is undeniable, we should not hesitate to proclaim it to the praise of God Who is glorified in His Saints, and for the benefit of the Faithful whose confidence is reanimated by these prodigies."

For those who still call themselves Christians, to deny the existence of the supernatural, would seem to be peculiarly inconsistent. The history of the chosen people was highly fraught with mysticism. Yet it was foretold that it should be a special characteristic of the New Dispensation that "your sons and daughters shall prophesy; your old men shall dream dreams, and your young men shall see visions. Moreover, upon My servants and handmaids in those days I will pour forth My Spirit."

It was on the Day of Pentecost that this prediction was perfectly accomplished. The Holy Ghost came down upon the Church to dwell with her and abide with her for ever. Jesus Christ then communicated to His chosen ones some portion of the Divine virtue which had ever resided in Himself. He had walked upon the waters as on dry land; He had calmed the tempest by a word, and hushed the angry sea by the mere exercise of His Will. He had multiplied food, feeding five thousand men with five barley loaves and two small fishes. At the Marriage Feast He had changed water into wine. He had escaped from the midst of His enemies by rendering Himself invisible to their eyes. Again and again He had cured the sick, and shown His power over the grave by restoring to health and strength those who had gone to that land from which it is said that none shall return to this. He had read the thoughts of men as one reads an open book, and the future was ever present to His gaze.

This mysterious power over nature Our Lord did not take away with Him altogether when He ascended to the Right Hand of God His Father; He bequeathed it as a precious inheritance to the Holy Church, which is His very Body. The Incarnation of the Word is a still -continuing, still – energizing fact. Emmanuel, God with us, still lives His Human Life in the Blessed Sacrament. In His last discourse, before withdrawing His visible presence from our midst, He appealed to His wonderful works in confirmation of His Divine Mission, and declared that they should last in even more abundant measure after His departure hence. Thus upon those made one with Him by sacramental union, does He from time to time bestow His gifts in proportion to their capacity for receiving these supernatural communications. To such Charismata the Apostle Saint Paul refers in the first Epistle to the Corinthians. Some are purely esoteric, for the sanctification of the individual; others are exoteric, for the edification of his neighbour. With these last we are alone concerned at the present moment. They have been with His Church from the beginning, and shall never leave her, so long as the world may run its course.

In vision the Prince of the Apostles learned that he should call nothing common or unclean which God had cleansed. In vision the Apostle of the Gentiles was converted to the Faith." In vision the Beloved Disciple witnessed "the Holy City Jerusalem coming down out of Heaven from God," and was permitted to behold the celestial worship of the Eternal. In vision the first Martyr saw Jesus standing at the Right Hand of God. In the New Testament we may read already that which we shall find repeated in the lives of the Saints of the after time. The Spirit of the Lord conveyed Saint Philip the Deacon mysteriously through the air to Azotus after he had baptized the Ethiopian eunuch in the desert that is between Jerusalem and Gaza. Saint Peter was delivered miraculously by an Angel from Herod's prison through the iron gate, which of itself opened to him and his heavenly guide. Already he had healed Eneas and raised Tabitha from the dead. The sick had been cured even by his passing shadow, as afterwards they were healed through "the handkerchiefs and aprons brought from the body" of his brother-Apostle, the great Saint Paul, who himself tells us that he was rapt in ecstasy and "caught up to the third Heaven; whether in the body or out of the body" he knew not. God alone knew the mystery.

Visions, ecstasies, the gift of tongues, the reading of hearts, the raising of the dead to life, miracles of all kinds we find in abundance in the

Apostolic Church. Nor did they cease with the days of the Apostles. Jesus Christ is the same yesterday, today, and for ever, and as is the Bridegroom, so is His Bride, the Holy Church, clothed with His Mantle as with a raiment of beauty, endowed with gifts from on high. Men may know her in every age not merely by her likeness to the divine original but by her oneness with Him. All things else may change. The Church of the Immutable changeth not. The spiritual children of the Apostles knew that they were heirs to the Apostolic gifts.

Saint Irenseus, in the second century, declared that there were then in the Church those who foresaw the future unfolded before their gaze. Origen proclaimed as a matter of personal knowledge, to the truth of which he called God to witness, that many Pagans had become Christians in consequence of the visions that they had received. This great man tells us that the Holy Ghost completely changed the hearts and minds of those early converts to the Faith, so that – at once instructed and fortified by the Divine communications, which had been bestowed upon them, sometimes in sleep, sometimes during their waking hours – they were ready to die for a doctrine which until then they had held in abhorrence.

But it was especially amongst the anchorites of the third century, that we find this Mystic Life most highly developed. In the lives of the Fathers of the Desert we see man by dint of contemplation and continual penance regaining his long-lost sovereignty, and wielding once more the sceptre of unfallen Adam over the animal creation; in these lives we perceive the gift of prophecy in fullest use; we see a Saint like Saint Antony beholding in vision the soul of Amnon ascending into Heaven at what was afterwards discovered to be the very moment of his death, at a distance represented by thirteen days' journey; we find the discernment of spirits insisted on by Saint Paul of old – the wiles of Satan discovered, and the ways of God recognized to His greater Glory; we learn how some of these holy men passed their days, as is related of Saint Macarius of Egypt, in almost continual ecstasy. Thus of the Abbot Sisois, it is told that he was ravished in ecstasy as soon as he lifted his hands in prayer. Therefore, when he prayed in company with his brethren, in his humility he would never raise his arms at all lest he should be suddenly rapt out of himself unawares. Again we read that a disciple of the Anchorite Sylvanus, on coming to visit him one day, found him in an ecstasy. He returned six hours, nine hours, and ten hours afterwards, always to find him in this same state. When at last Sylvanus came back to earthly life, he said that he had seen the Glory of God revealed to his enraptured gaze.

We need hardly say that we quote these examples, taken out of a multitude, not as though we wished to claim credence for any one particular fact, but simply with the desire to show that the Church of God is always the same in her mysterious life on earth. Visions, prophecies, miracles, are no new things in her wondrous story. In her Saints, the Redeemer's promise will be ever verified, that they should do even greater works than it had pleased Him to accomplish while he was dwelling as the Son of Man, visibly, in the midst of His people.

She is the city set upon a hill – visible to all who

will recognize her Divine Credentials. Surely, then, one of the signs that mark out the true Church of Christ from all beside her is her identity in every period of the world's history. Here is true continuity. The continuity not of barren titles and rich emoluments, but of oneness of life. We see not merely the organism and the functions of the Apostolic Church intact, but even the marvellous spiritual endowments, so freely granted in the beginning, in the possession of her Saints in every age. In the last century, not a few of the gifts bestowed by God in the first days of the Faith are beheld again in such a life-story as that of Saint Gerard Majella. We have seen them reproduced in no limited measure in our own times in holy Priests like the Blessed Cure d'Ars, and Don Bosco of Turin.

At the beginning of the twentieth century, we are living at a time when physical forces in nature, hitherto but little suspected by the many, seem to be gradually coming to light. It is certain also that the powers of evil are busily engaged in many a spiritualistic seance in a very parody of the Communion of Saints. Simon Magus followed close in the wake of Simon Peter, and when Faith goes out by the door, superstition always comes in by the window.

In these days, then, of thought-reading, clairvoyance, telepathy, hypnotism, and of what is vaguely called "occult science," there is little doubt but that men in general will be less disposed idly to scoff at such phenomena as are to be found in the lives of the Saints, than would have been the case even a few years ago. But there still remains much gross materialism to be combated all around us, and it is now even more necessary than was ever before the case to distinguish the false from the true, the dross from the gold, the diabolic from the Divine. This can only effectually be done by the study of mystical theology, and of the lives of the Saints in a Catholic spirit, and with that fear of the Lord which we know to be the beginning of wisdom. The contemplation of the miraculous will surely be most profitable to our souls if it deepens our faith in God, and our confidence in the powerful intercession of His glorious Servants.

The Life of Saint Gerard was not merely full of marvel, but is also rich in practical lessons. If anyone wishes to be convinced of this, he need only turn to his resolutions, or again to his letter to the Superior of a convent, to see how far Brother Gerard was from being aught of an empty dreamer. His steps were ever upon the earth, although he walked in the presence of God, and his heart was where his Treasure was – in Heaven. He knew well that there is only one royal road to sanctity – conformity to the Will of God, by the faithful discharge of the duties of one's state – be they small or be they great – out of love for Jesus Christ our Blessed Lord.

"Some," he would often say, "place sanctity in this; some in that. For my part, I place it only in doing the Will of God."

Those who may wish to learn more of Saint Gerard than it has been possible to tell them in the compass of this little book are advised to procure his life, written by Father Tannoia, and published in the Oratorian Series of the Lives of the Saints, in the volume entitled, "The First Companions of Saint Alphonsus."

In everything that he has here written, the writer need hardly say that he submits himself to the Holy Roman See, of which it is his supreme joy and consolation to profess himself to be always, and in all things, a most obedient, loyal son.

— Father Oliver Rodie Vassall-Philips, C.Ss.R.
Saint Joseph's, Kingswood, Bristol, England

HIS CHILDHOOD

About fifty miles south of Naples the traveller will come upon the picturesque little town of Muro. Nestling snugly amidst the Apennines, it looks down from the mountain slopes upon a wide expanse of fertile plain, which stretches away beneath its walls.

Muro is an Episcopal See. Like most Italian cities, it is rich in religious houses. Here especially the children of Saint Francis are to be found in large numbers. You may mark their humble homes, as they rise in unadorned simplicity, beside buildings of great architectural beauty.

It was in this pleasant spot, favoured alike by nature and grace, that God was pleased to place the cradle of Saint Gerard. His father was a man of lowly birth, a tailor by trade, but full of piety and virtue. Upon this worthy man – Dominic Majella was his name – Heaven bestowed first two daughters and then a son, the story of whose short but marvellous life we are about to present to our readers. This boy was born on the 6th of April, in the year 1726, and was baptized by the name of

Gerard on the very day of his birth, in the cathedral of his native city.

God is wonderful in all His Saints. Yet it is true that these His chosen servants show forth His Goodness and Wisdom in widely differing ways. This must necessarily be the case, since widely different are the purposes that they are designed to effect in the varied story of the Church's warfare. According to the need, so is the gift bestowed. Some of the greatest of the Saints have mirrored the Divine Perfections by the spotlessness of their souls in the ordinary discharge of everyday duties. Their virtues were heroic, but it was not necessary to their vocation that they should receive many extraordinary prerogatives. Others on the contrary have preached the Infinite Power of God, even on the housetops, by the marvellous miracles that He has enabled them to perform, or rather that He has Himself deigned to perform at their prayer and through their instrumentality. To this latter class belongs our Saint Gerard.

His life was one long wonder. In him God seems to have delighted to stultify the shallow eighteenth century in which his lot was cast. The long series of his miracles furnish by themselves a sufficient answer to the sneer of infidels, not merely of his own time, but also of the present day.

It is idle to proclaim theoretically, that something cannot take place, to those who have seen it actually occur before their very eyes. Thus no man who watched the doings of Saint Gerard could doubt the possibility of miracles, for Gerard worked miracles all his life through, and that continually and often under circumstances of much publicity. For this reason alone the story of his life is full of useful teaching for a materialistic age. It breathes the supernatural as its native air. In the world, but never of the world, he seems a visitant from the everlasting shores, come for a little while to dwell in our midst. Such a life as his tells silently of the Invisible Presence which ever governs all we see around us. It is meant to burn into our minds and hearts in letters of fire the remembrance of the Sovereignty of God.

In writing this little sketch of Saint Gerard, we can only state some few of his miracles. Should anyone wish to study in detail the proofs on which they rest, we would refer him to the testimony adduced in the Processes of his Beatification. If evidence such as this, given on oath by a mass of witnesses in every way worthy of credence, be rejected as inconclusive, it is hard to see what would be accepted as satisfactory.

In Gerard's early childhood Our Lord was, in His wonderful condescension, pleased to make free with him in ways most strange and lovely. Thus we are told that, when he was but five years old, he went one day to a chapel in a hamlet called Capotignano, a little more than a mile outside of Muro, where is venerated an image of Our Blessed Lady holding the Divine Child in her arms. No sooner had the boy knelt down to say his prayers, than He who tells us that His delights are to be with the children of men, seemed to descend from His Mother's arms, a smile upon his lips, and commenced to play familiarly with little Gerard. Then after a while the Holy Child gave Gerard, as a pledge of his love, a tiny loaf of exceeding whiteness. (Miracles, however extraordinary, are not, as a general rule, isolated in the lives of the Saints.

Thus it is interesting to note that we find a miracle very similar to this recorded in the account of the early childhood of Blessed Hermann Joseph.)

When Gerard reached home, he was, as we may well imagine, brimming over with innocent happiness. Without delay he brought his wonderful present to his mother in the gladness of his heart. She was naturally much surprised, and asked the boy who had given him the bread.

"It was," he answered, "the Child of a beautiful lady with whom I have been playing."

For many succeeding days this miracle was renewed. Drawn by the heavenly attraction of the Divine Child of Bethlehem, each morning Gerard went to the shrine of Capotignano, and each morning did the prodigy recur. On one occasion his sister Bridget followed him at a safe distance, and was an eye-witness of the magic scene.

In later years, after he had become a Redemptorist, when this same sister came one day to see him, Gerard said to her with his usual simplicity:

"Now I understand that it was the Infant Jesus who used to give me those beautiful little loaves."

"Very well," replied his sister with a smile, "let us then go and visit Him once more."

"No," said Gerard, "for now I can find Him everywhere, whenever I please."

This holy child, already so dear to the Sacred Heart of Jesus, was not seven years old when already his soul yearned for the Bread that cometh down from Heaven. One day during Mass the little boy felt a secret inspiration to go up with the people and receive Holy Communion. The priest, seeing that he was hardly more than a baby in appearance, passed him by. The child went back to his place in the church, the tears flowing down his cheeks. But the next night the great Archangel Saint Michael came to console him, bearing the body of his Lord. This miraculous Communion was, doubtless, one of the great reasons for Saint Gerard's life-long devotion to the Prince of the Angelic Hosts.

Sent to school at an early age, Gerard's virtues soon made him very dear both to master and boys. All wondered at his extraordinary piety. His devotion to the Blessed Sacrament and to Our Blessed Lady increased day by day. At this period of his life, we are told that, during the solemn time which elapses in the Holy Mass between the Consecration and the Priest's Communion, the Infant Jesus often appeared to the boy's enraptured gaze upon the Altar.

His, however, was no morbid or unreal devotion. This was proved by his constant and unfailing charity, the one touchstone of all true sanctity. Full of the love of God, and ever anxious to help those in trouble in any way he might, Gerard grew daily in grace, until at the age of ten his confessor permitted him to go every other day to Holy Communion. After his death his good mother, speaking of the childhood of her dear son, expressed herself as follows:

"My child found his only pleasure in the church, on his knees before the Blessed Sacrament. He used to remain there so long that he would forget the dinner-hour. In the house, young as he was, he prayed all day. He was born for Heaven."

Happy mother of such a son!

HIS APPRENTICESHIP TO A TRADE

W hen Gerard had left Muro and was living in a boarding-school hard by, he received the news of his father's death. His mother now found herself in somewhat straitened circumstances, and was compelled to remove her son from school. She apprenticed him to a tailor called Pannuto. Here the holy boy gave himself heart and soul to his work, but was careful at the same time to correspond faithfully with the inspirations from on high, which drew him irresistibly to the interior life.

Oftentimes, whilst his fingers plied the needle, his spirit was rapt in God. Already from time to time he was ravished in ecstasy.

It was also his custom to hide himself underneath the work-table in order the more freely to pour forth his heart, unobserved by men, in fervent prayer. His master, Pannuto, loved him, and recognizing his virtues, would not check these extraordinary impulses of Divine Grace. But this was not the case with the foreman, a person of violent temper, who could not understand our Saint. One day he dragged him from the place where he was praying, and belaboured him with blows.

"Strike! strike!" cried Gerard. "Well you may; you have cause enough."

On another occasion this tyrant struck the victim of his brutality with such violence that he fell swooning to the ground. Suddenly Pannuto appeared on the scene and demanded an explanation. The foreman did not know what to reply, but relying, as the event proved with good reason, on Gerard's unfailing charity, he stammered out:

"He knows: let him tell you himself."

The Saint meekly replied with perfect truth that he had fallen off his tailor's table, keeping to himself the cause of that cruel fall.

Gerard had even after this to suffer unceasing insults and blows from his savage tormentor. He bore them all with a smile, forgiving his persecutor, in whom he recognized the unsuspecting instrument of the Will of God. Well did he know that these sufferings were intended to be the great instrument of his sanctification by forming in him the Christian character; by making him more and more gentle, meek, humble, and forgiving – in a word, rendering him more and more like Christ his Lord, who, when He was reviled, answered not again, and gladly endured unspeakable indignities at the hands of sinners.

Meanwhile, God was preparing a respite for his servant. One day Pannuto followed him secretly to the church, and was there entranced by the spectacle that met his gaze. After having prayed for some time with great fervour, Gerard performed an act of mortification and humility that is much practised by the people of Southern

Italy – an act which Saint Alphonsus used to en-
courage them to perform in reparation for the
blasphemy that is unfortunately too common
amongst impulsive Neapolitans. He prostrated
himself, kissed the ground, and drew his tongue
along the pavement until he came to the foot of
the Altar. He was then immediately ravished in an
ecstasy.

This scene made a lasting impression upon
Pannuto. Amazed to see his young apprentice admitted by God to such a lofty state of contemplation, thenceforth he venerated him as a Saint, and
dismissed his persecutor.

At this period Almighty God was pleased to
work the following great miracle through Saint
Gerard. The servant of God was one night with his
master's son guarding his vineyards against possible
thieves. In order the better to enkindle his devotion
towards the Passion of Our Lord, Gerard made a
cross, surrounded it with some lights, and commenced to chant the Miserere. Suddenly some
ricks of straw took fire.

Pannuto's son cried out in alarm.

"It is nothing," said Gerard, and, as he made
the sign of the cross, the fire was at once extin-
guished.

Our Saint was still in Pannuto's service when,
on the Feast of Pentecost in the year 1740, he received the Sacrament of Confirmation at the
hands of the Bishop of Lacedogna, acting on behalf of the Bishop of the diocese. At this time
Gerard was fourteen years of age. Henceforth he
would seem to have contracted a most intimate
union in the depths of his soul with the Holy Spirit
of God. A special devotion to the Holy Ghost was

always one of the marked characteristics of his piety.

Whenever in future life his advice was asked on any subject, he was accustomed to invoke first the aid of the All-wise Spirit of God. This pious habit was no doubt the source of the unfailing prudence of the counsel that he gave – sometimes in cases of no ordinary difficulty.

On finishing his apprenticeship with Pannuto, his mother placed him in the house of another tailor named Vitus Mennona. Here he was remarkable for his great spirit of prayer, obedience, and charity, so that his master acquired a veneration for the servant of God which lasted until his holy death. In his old age Mennona used to journey to the Redemptorist house where Gerard was living, and would there pour forth his soul, speaking with the greatest enthusiasm of the virtues of the holy Brother.

But the young lover of the Crucified thought himself too comfortable with the good Mennona. He felt an irresistible attraction to the Religious Life. Accordingly, presenting himself at a convent of Capuchins in the neighbourhood – where he had an uncle, a Father Bonaventure, a theologian of distinction – he craved admission as a postulant for the habit of Saint Francis. But his youth and the wretched state of his health caused him to be refused, the Superiors judging that his request came rather from a passing movement of fervour than from a Divine vocation.

That he might somewhat console his nephew for this refusal, Father Bonaventure gave him a new suit of clothes, which, as we read, he sadly wanted, and then sent him away. At the very door of the convent he happened to meet a poor beggar in rags, who asked an alms for the love of God. Touched at the sight of his misery, Gerard at once took off his new clothes, and gave them to the poor man. Father Bonaventure, however, on being told this, did not quite like the way that his present had been treated, and sent for the culprit to express his displeasure.

"Oh, my dear uncle," said the Saint, "do not, I entreat you, be put out with me! The beggar to whom I gave your clothes needed them far more than I did. Had you yourself seen that poor brother of Jesus Christ, you would have been the first to give them to him."

Father Bonaventure could say no more. He thanked God in his heart for having taught his nephew thus to love the poor, so dear to Our Divine Lord.

HIS TRIALS AND VOCATION

Having been refused admittance into their Order by the Capuchins, Saint Gerard determined to wait some clearer call from God, and meanwhile to labour more assiduously than ever at the work of his sanctification. With this end in view, he engaged himself as servant to a gentleman whose temper was so notoriously ungovernable that no one could live a month in his employment. In the life of labour and humiliation which now opened out before his path, Gerard's heart rejoiced, for thus could he imitate Him, the Lord of Heaven, Who appeared as a servant for our sake. Indeed, the thought of the humility and meekness of Our Blessed Saviour in the midst of His dread sufferings was his one comfort in his new surroundings.

He was only sixteen years of age, and the poor boy was the butt for all the concentrated spleen of his ill-humoured master. Multiplied orders, reproaches heaped upon him without cause, interminable scoldings, threats that he would be turned out of the house – such were the lot of Gerard from the very commencement. People wondered how he could bear it all; but he used to say gently that his master was his best friend, and that for his own part he had no other thought than that of remaining faithfully in his service.

He lived a life of the greatest personal austerity. His ordinary food was dry bread. A few vegetables he looked upon as a luxurious banquet. Everything that he could save from the food provided for his own meals he used to give to the poor. All his spare time he was accustomed to pass in the presence of Our Lord in the Blessed Sacrament.

It was at this period that it pleased God to reward the fidelity of His servant by another great miracle. One day, his master having gone out for a walk, Gerard locked the door of his apartments, carried off the key, and proceeded to fetch some water from the well in the public square. While leaning over the kerb, by some mishap the precious key slipped from his grasp and fell into the well below.

"What will my master say?" cried he in uttermost consternation. "What a state he will be in!"

One first moment of dismay! Then, from the very bottom of his heart he asked the help of God. Suddenly there came an inspiration. Running quickly to the Cathedral sacristy, he flew back with a little statue of the Infant Jesus in his hands. The bystanders, who were witnesses of the scene, waited, all expectation, to see what might come next. Amidst a general silence Gerard addressed Our Lord with much simplicity, begging Him to restore the lost key.

Soon he was seen to tie the statue to a string. Down it went lower and lower into the well. For an instant all was suspense. Then behold once more the statue reappeared, bearing the key in triumph to its happy owner! No wonder that such a miracle as this was talked of for many a mile all the country round. Even to this day they will point out to you the well, which, in memory of the marvel, was henceforth to be known to all as Pozzo Gerardiello, or Gerard's well.

Our Saint had been now three years in the service of this hard taskmaster, when suddenly the tyrant died. Far from experiencing any feeling of relief, he mourned his loss as that of the best of friends and benefactors. So eager was he always to suffer for the love of Christ.

Saint Gerard now determined to return home and practise his trade of tailor. He was kept busily occupied during the day. A great part of the night he spent in the Cathedral in presence of the Blessed Sacrament. Indeed, his was already a life of the most heroic sanctity. Knowing well that almsdeeds and fasting are the wings that waft our prayers to Heaven and make them acceptable in the sight of God, he divided all the money he received into three equal portions. One part he gave to his mother for the support of the house, another he devoted to the poor, and the remaining third was a loving alms for Masses, wherewith to comfort the Holy Souls in Purgatory.

He also redoubled his corporal penances, taking the discipline with great severity, and in general treating his body with the utmost rigour. At this time, thinking constantly of Jesus Who allowed Himself to be as a fool in the court of Herod, Saint Gerard feigned madness in the streets, and rejoiced when he was treated with contumely as a simpleton by the boys of his native town. Truly love – the love of the Saints for God – is strong as death and stronger than life itself. Gerard would, had it been possible, have set the whole world ablaze with the fire of charity that God had enkindled in his own affectionate heart. Oftentimes he would, as though constrained by some uncontrollable impulse, call out to his mother, his sisters, or his friends:

"Come! let us go together and visit Jesus in the Blessed Sacrament. Is He not there, our Prisoner of Love?"

The Sacred Heart of Jesus drew Gerard's heart very close to Itself.

To this burning love for Our Blessed Lord, he joined the tenderest devotion to Mary, the gentle Mother of God. When he found himself before one of the images of Our Lady, he could hardly tear himself from the spot. He loved to say again and again:

"The Madonna has stolen away my heart, and for my part I have made her a present of it."

Once when they were celebrating at Muro a novena in honour of the Immaculate Conception, Gerard remained for a long time on his knees in fervent prayer before an image of the sinless Queen of Heaven. Then suddenly in sight of all the people he rose, and, like Saint Edmund of Canterbury long centuries before, placing a ring on the finger of the statue, cried aloud:

"See, I am espoused to the Madonna!" Thus would he publicly proclaim that he had conse-crated the pearl of his virginity to the glorious Virgin Mother.

Gerard was now twenty-two years of age, when at length it pleased Divine Providence to open for him the door to the Religious State.

In 1749 the Redemptorist Fathers gave a mission at Muro. Gerard had already, in the previous year, expressed his longing to enter the Congregation of the most Holy Redeemer as a Lay-brother; and now he renewed his entreaties with even greater earnestness than before.

However, at first the same fate that befell him with the Capuchins came to test his confidence in God. Father Cafaro, Rector of the House at Iliceto, was among the missioners at Muro. He noticed the delicacy of Gerard's appearance, and thought him to be but ill-suited for the hard life of a Lay-brother. On this ground he felt himself bound to meet our Saint's petition with a positive refusal.

Meanwhile Gerard's mother and sister on their side were by no means idle. They shrank from the very idea of losing him, and as they knew that, notwithstanding the obstacles he had encountered, he was far from giving up his project in despair, they locked him up, as they thought safely, in his room. But the prisoner cut up his bedclothes, and with their help let himself down from the window, leaving behind a note to say that he had gone away to make himself a saint!

He now pursued the Redemptorist Fathers to a place called Rionero, where they had gone to give a mission, and renewed his request in the most humble and touching manner possible. Once more refused, he exclaimed:

"Do but try me. This is all that I ask. You can send me away afterwards if you please."

Seeing that they were still determined not to accept him, he threw himself on his knees and, crying bitterly, declared that if he were refused admittance into the convent, he would be found every morning outside its doors begging alms with the poor. This firmness of purpose touched Father Cafaro to the heart. He made up his mind to give Gerard the trial he craved so earnestly. Accordingly he sent him to Iliceto with a note to the acting-Superior of the House, in which he said simply:

"I send you a useless Brother."

Saint Alphonsus has written the life of Father Cafaro, and left us his testimony to the exceptional sanctity of the great servant of God whom he knew so well. But even Father Cafaro could not foresee how warmly God would espouse the cause of the new postulant. That frail frame was to be so strengthened, that, in the discharge of the daily duties of his laborious state, he should always prove one of the most useful members of any community to which he might be attached. But this in the future.

For the moment he was only "a useless Brother."

HIS NOVICIATE

G erard, duly armed with Father Cafaro's little note of introduction, proceeded in all haste to the Redemptorist House at Iliceto. Situated in a solitude rather more than a mile outside the little town, this convent had originally been built by the Blessed Felix of Corsano for the Augustinians, but it had been abandoned by them some time before it was accepted by Saint Alphonsus as a home for his Religious. The House was always very dear to the holy Founder, who loved it especially because of an ancient and miraculous picture of the Blessed Virgin, venerated under the title of Our Lady of Consolation, which was preserved in the church attached to the convent. It was here that Saint Alphonsus wrote his first book, the well-known Visits to the Blessed Sacrament, and it was here that Gerard was to spend the greater part of his short Religious Life.

He had hardly been a few days in the house before it became evident that the new Brother was a model of every virtue. As soon then as the Father Rector returned home, he was told that the postulant whom he had sent to Iliceto, far from being "useless," as he had feared would be the case, was on the contrary the greatest blessing to the whole Community. Gerard was soon after this admitted formally into the Noviciate, and given the holy Habit of Religion.

Never, surely, had there been seen a more fervent novice. If his life in the world had been most admirable, his life in the cloister was still more so. According to the testimony of the other Brothers, he managed by himself to do the work of four. At the same time, none knew so well as he how to unite the contemplative to the active life, by making every external occupation one long prayer, an act of unbroken homage to the Majesty of God.

He never forgot Who was the Master that it was his privilege to serve in the Religious State. The convent in which he dwelt was in his eyes the Palace of the great King. In the sunshine of His real Presence in the midst of His Own, Gerard found the supreme happiness of his life, and his loyal heart rejoiced to do fealty to his Lord not only in word but also in deed, "in much patience, in labours, in watchings, in fastings, in sweetness, in the Holy Ghost, in charity unfeigned."

For a short time he was employed in the garden. This kind of manual labour must have been strange and hard enough for the young tailor. But he never complained. On the contrary, he used to do the work of others in addition to his own, saying with a smile on his face:

"Let me do it. I am the youngest. Do you please rest yourselves awhile."

The more humble the nature of the duty assigned to him, the better was he pleased. Deeply rooted in humility, he had taken labour for his bride, and was never happy when separated from her. We may say at once that this was one of the most marked characteristics of Saint Gerard's sanctity throughout life. His at least was no dreamy, useless, or unpractical existence.

The mysterious mastery that we shall see him exercising again and again over the inanimate creation and the hidden forces of nature, God seems to have given to Saint Gerard, as to Saint Francis and to many of his first children, in reward for the purity of heart by which they almost returned to that state of "Original Justice," when Man, before sin had torn the sceptre from his grasp, was in very truth Lord of all creation. But this perfect purity of spirit, this undimmed clearness of vision, which was theirs in such perfection that, for them, Nature seems to have raised her veil that thus she might disclose the powers of the unseen world behind her, could be purchased only at the price of a complete self-mastery, and heroic mortification of all that is merely of this earth earthly, and of the senses sensible. This recovery, at least in part, of the rightful dominion in the Universe, which Man lost in the beginning by his first great Fall, is one of the unforeseen consequences resulting in God's goodness, from the austerity of the Saints, often to their own confusion – an austerity that sometimes appalls us by the dread determination of its ceaseless self-crucifixion.

It may be asserted without any fear of exaggeration that amongst all the Saints hardly will one be found more austere or more devoted to corporal penances than was Saint Gerard Majella; yet at the same time he well understood that the austerity which holds the first place before God, and which

is most acceptable in His sight, is the austerity that
leads us to the faithful discharge of the duties of
our state, always sparing others whenever possible,
never sparing ourselves. Well did he know that
without this vivifying spirit, issuing forth from the
Heart of Jesus, the mortifications even of the Bap-
tist in the desert, or of Saint Simeon on his pillar,
would have been as sounding brass or a tinkling
symbol.

(An all-embracing, all-pervading spirit of self-
sacrifice – the mortification of the whole being, not
only of the pleasures of sense, but much more of
the will, for the love of God and man, is the domi-
nant note of Christian asceticism. This it is that
differentiates it from the purely external austerities
of the Fakir or the Dervish, which too often are but
an emanation of the subtle spirit of pride and con-
tempt for the rest of men, by which they are held
in bondage. The asceticism of the Saints derived
all its energy from an insatiable longing, that grew
with their growth in its power and intensity to become more and more conformable to the Likeness
of the Crucified Lover of our race; it was animated
not merely by a desire to safeguard personal salvation, but also by the knowledge that thus they
might help effectually those – their brothers and
their sisters in the world-wide family of God – for
whom Jesus had shed His Precious Blood. If Saint
Paul tells us that he chastised his body lest he might
after all become a castaway (I Corinthians 9:27), in
another place he writes, "I fill up in my body those
things that are wanting of the sufferings of Christ,
for His Body's sake, which is the Church." (Colos-
sians 1:24) The law of love must ever be also the
law of self-immolation in behalf of the beloved.

The false asceticism of fanatics is the fruit of a dark unlovely pessimism that withers all it touches. Sane asceticism, on the other hand, that which alone we see blessed and canonized by the Church, is the inevitable outgrowth of the only perfect optimism – springing from the Heaven-sent Faith in a world saved by sacrifice on the hill of Calvary through the Death of the Son of God for man.)

Saint Gerard always remains – especially, no doubt, for those called, like himself, to the Religious State, but also for all who will study' his life – a most perfect model of hard-working charity. Those who "live laborious days," as did Brother Gerard, and who, like him, are ever kind to all they meet, will become, like him, dear to God and dear to their fellow-men.

So great, in truth, was his meekness, so devoted and self-forgetful his life, that it used to be said of him in the Noviciate: "Either this Brother is a fool, or he is a great Saint." Verily Gerard was a Saint indeed, captivated with the holy folly of the Cross of Christ.

Saint Gerard was not long left in charge of the garden. Soon he was given the more congenial office of Sacristan. We may easily imagine with what joy he undertook duties that brought him so continually into the immediate presence of that Lord Who was the only love of his heart. Fifty years after the death of the holy Brother, people still spoke with admiration of the care which he lavished on all that related to the House of God. The taste with which he adorned the altars, especially on great Feasts, was the subject of general admiration. His whole heart was in his work. His one thought was to beautify the place where Jesus dwells, his one great trouble that any should be found to neglect visiting the Most Blessed Sacrament.

For his own part, every spare moment was spent before the Tabernacle. Father Tannoia, the venerable biographer of Saint Alphonsus, tells us that once he chanced to be in a part of the church where he could not be seen by anyone, when he observed the holy Brother pause and kneel down before the altar. Then he commenced, as it were, to wrestle with himself, as though he would fain steal away from some powerful attraction. After some moments of effort, as if he were still unable to escape, he – thinking that no one else was present – cried out aloud:

"O Lord, let me go, I pray Thee! I have work that I must do."

Then obedience and duty triumphed in his soul. He tore himself away from the embraces of his God. Such is the love of the Saints for Jesus hidden in the Most Holy Sacrament.

Hand in hand with the love of Jesus goes the love of Mary His Blessed Mother. The zeal of Saint Gerard, worthy son of Saint Alphonsus, to spread abroad confidence in the Holy Mother of God, literally knew no bounds. Not content with fasting rigorously during the novenas that precede her feasts, it was his invariable custom to spend the last night, as a vigil of devotion, in prayer before one of her images or pictures. He was never more happy than when arranging some grand procession in honour of his heavenly Mother; and by every means in his power he strove to propagate her "healthful worship."

The Saints set much store on things which to

the thoughtless seem of but small account. Thus
we are told that it was one of Gerard's great delights to distribute far and wide rosaries and scapu-
lars of Our Blessed Lady. He knew well that, where
the rosary is said devoutly, there the Sacraments
will be frequented, and the people will grow in the
fear and the love of God, while the pious wearing
of the holy scapular is the pledge of the special
protection of that dear Mother, who never will
permit any of her faithful children to die at enmity
with her Divine Son.

Thus, full of love for Jesus and Mary, the holy
Brother seemed more like a seraph of Heaven than
an inhabitant of this dull earth of ours. So evident
to all was his extraordinary sanctity, that Saint
Alphonsus gladly shortened in his behalf the time
ordinarily required as a period of probation for a
Lay-brother in the Congregation, permitting him
to be admitted to Profession on July 16, in the year
1752.

Inexpressible was the joy of his heart. Henceforth he belonged exclusively to God, his Saviour,
to whose perpetual service he had bound himself
by the golden chains of the Holy Vows. Henceforth, dead to the things of time, he was to live for
God alone. Stripped of all things earthly, and
nailed to the cross with Christ his Master, he offered himself, without reserve, as an oblation to the
Most High. His sacrifice was accepted and repaid a
hundredfold by Him Who never permits Himself
to be outdone in generosity. God looked into the
heart of His son, saw that it was empty of self, and
filled it, even to overflowing, with the gift of His
holy love.

HIS EXTRAORDINARY GIFTS

S ome little time before Saint Gerard's Profession, Father Cafaro ceased to be Rector at Iliceto. He was succeeded by Father Fiocchi. It was during Father Fiocchi's Rectorate that the holy Brother commenced the long series of prodigies, terminated only by death, which entitle him to rank in the splendour of supernatural endowments with such marvellous Saints as Saint Joseph Cupertino and Christian the Wonderful.

Some of the events that we are about to relate are indeed of an astounding character, but they all rest upon incontrovertible evidence; they all, or almost all, can be paralleled in the Lives of the Saints, and they all preach, in a tongue that the most obtuse can hardly fail to understand, the Sovereign Power of the Lord our God, Who was pleased in this mysterious manner to exalt, even here below, His humble and faithful servant.

One day when Gerard was out walking with two young countrymen, they came upon a church dedicated to the Holy Mother of God. The Saint at once welcomed the opportunity of speaking to his companions on the incomparable dignity of

Our Blessed Lady. Scarcely had the sweet Name of Mary fallen from his lips, than his countenance appeared aflame, and he seemed as one transfigured. Then, taking a pencil and a piece of paper, he wrote something and threw it into the air, as though it were a letter addressed to the Queen of Heaven. A vigorous bound accompanied this singular action, and immediately there ensued what is called by writers of Mystical Theology the Ecstatic Flight. His companions suddenly saw him raised from the ground in their presence, and miraculously carried through the air for more than half a mile.

Gerard came down to earth again only to work a fresh miracle, this time a miracle of charity and healing. On reaching the door of his convent, he found awaiting his return a young man with a gangrened leg. This poor sufferer had with great difficulty been brought to Iliceto, that he might there in person recommend himself to the prayers of the Servant of God, the fame of whose sanctity had been now widely noised abroad. No sooner did he see Gerard than he cried out sobbing that he could no longer labour for his daily bread, and was thus compelled, against his will, to lead the life of a beggar. Touched to the heart, the Saint asked to see the diseased leg. It was swathed round and round with bandages.

Saint Gerard carefully removed the wraps, and perceived at once that the flesh was being eaten away by a frightful cancer. Then, calling to mind the example set him by great Servants of God, who had in their own day performed this same miracle of charity, he applied his lips to the wound and commenced to suck forth all its venom.

Our Lord is not wont to leave such heroism as this without its due reward.

"Confidence in God, my brother," cried the Saint; "you will soon be well again."

He then carefully dried the sore place, and bandaged it with clean linen. At that moment the pain ceased. The young man, full of thankfulness and joy, cast himself at the feet of Gerard to thank him for his great goodness, calling him a saint from on high and an angel – messenger sent by God's loving – kindness to His children. But the holy Brother would have no thanks. The thanks were due to God alone. Let him show his gratitude by leading a truly virtuous life for the time to come. However, the poor man was not to be stayed. When next morning he found that his leg was perfectly healed, he proclaimed his wonderful cure to all he met, so that the whole town soon rang with the news.

It was not so long after entering the Congregation that Brother Gerard, though Sacristan at the time, was directed to see to the wants of four young clerics who were making their Retreat in the house in preparation for ordination. In the discharge of this duty he went one day to the strangers' refectory to prepare the table for dinner. Now, in this refectory, hung a picture of Our Lord represented as the Ecce Homo. The moment that Gerard's eyes met those of his Divine Master, they were immovably fixed; his arms became extended; his body was motionless as a corpse. He remained, as though lifeless, in the position in which he had been overcome by the visitation of God, a fork in one hand, a napkin in the other. Soon a second Lay-brother appeared on the scene. Noticing that the table was not yet laid, and that Gerard did not stir, he commenced to call him, but in vain. There was no answer, no sign of life. He was then naturally somewhat alarmed, and called some other Brothers to the spot. They all likewise began to try and awaken Gerard. All was to no purpose. At last the Father Rector was summoned. He shook the Servant of God by the arm, and gave him an "Obedience" to come to himself.

In his ecstasies, obedience was the only force that could recall him to this earth. So soon as obedience spoke, the ecstasy always ceased. This is the infallible sign of the good spirit, the one test by which the gift of God may be discerned from its diabolic counterfeit. On this occasion, in order to preserve Gerard in deep humility, and to guard him with the greatest security against all danger of delusion, the Father Rector gave the holy Brother a sharp rebuke, and told him to get to his work at once.

Saint Gerard, dumbfounded at being thus discovered, whilst in the unrestrained enjoyment of the intimacies of Heaven, accepted the reproof with joy. Blame he always looked upon as his due. In his own sight he was not worthy to be allowed to speak to God in lowly prayer, still less to be rapt in ecstatic contemplation. This he never coveted or sought in any way. But it would have been entirely beyond his power to withstand either in body or soul the imperious operations of the Holy Spirit of God. He could but leave himself as a passive instrument in his Creator's Hands.

This was not the only occasion that a mere glance at some representation of the Passion sufficed to throw him into an ecstasy. One Good Friday, the first after his Profession, a large picture of the Crucifixion was carried through the streets of the little town of Corato. Now Gerard chanced to be in Corato at the time, and when, in the course of its appointed route, the procession entered the Benedictine Church, it passed by the spot where he was on his knees in prayer.

At the thought of the sufferings of our Most Holy Redeemer, thus vividly brought before his sight, Saint Gerard was seized with an uncontrollable transport of heavenly love. He swooned away in ecstasy, and – in presence of all the assembled people – was raised off the earth a considerable distance above the ground, his gaze fixed steadfastly the while on the sorrowful Countenance of his Crucified Saviour.

As David danced before the Ark of the Ancient Covenant, so did Gerard, living under the New Law, sometimes manifest his joy in the far deeper consolations with which he was favoured by his Lord. A blind beggar came one day to the Convent, playing the flute and asking an alms. Gerard requested him to play the Italian air set to the words of the hymn written by Saint Alphonsus, beginning thus:

"Tis Thy good pleasure, not mine own,
In Thee, my God, I love alone;
And nothing I desire of Thee
But what Thy goodness wills for me –
O Will of God! O Will Divine!
All, all our love be ever Thine."

No sooner had the minstrel commenced, than an inebriation of heavenly love overcame Saint

Gerard. He suddenly commenced to dance and bound in the air, repeating over and over again:

"'Tis Thy good pleasure, not mine own,
In Thee, my God, I love alone."

Then all at once he raised himself from the ground with the rapidity of an arrow going straight to its mark, his eyes turned towards Heaven. He remained for some time absolutely unsupported in mid-air in an ecstasy of love.

On another occasion, in the course of conversation with Father Strina, a man well known for his devotion to the Divine Infant, Gerard said to him jokingly:

"You have no love for the Divine Infant."

"And you," retorted Father Strina, "you have no love for the Madonna."

This was too much for Saint Gerard. On the instant, taken out of himself by heavenly love, and strengthened with a supernatural strength, he seized on the astonished Father Strina and began to dance with him round and round, raising him from the ground with the ease with which one would raise a wisp of straw.

Thus was this humble Lay -brother, while yet detained on earth in the body of this death, freed from that control of the senses over the spirit, of matter over the freedom of heavenly contemplation, which ordinarily weighs poor mortals down beneath its weight during their sojourn here below. Gerard soared to Heaven, not only on the wings of the prayer of faith, but, by a rare privilege, he of-ten-times carried his body with him in his upward flight.

Another grace bestowed upon our Saint was his knowledge of events which had passed at a distance, and concerning which he had no natural means of information. He was thus supernaturally apprised of the tragic death of the Priest who had baptized him in infancy. This worthy ecclesiastic having been assassinated in the streets of Muro, Gerard, on the very day of the murder, told the sorrowful news to three of his fellow-citizens. Let one of them tell the story in his own words.

"I was at that time pursuing my studies in Naples," he writes, "and Gerard used often to come in the evening, and we would say our Rosary together. One night he seemed quite sad and crushed with despondency. I asked him the reason of his trouble.

"'My dear Pascal,' was his answer, 'I am grieved to think that our Archpriest has just been assassinated.'

"'Assassinated!' I rejoined, 'that is out of the question. It is only a few hours ago that I received a letter from home. They would have told me if that had happened.'

"However, Gerard persisted that there was no doubt about the fact, and I heard afterwards that the murder had been committed the very day on which he had assured me of its occurrence."

By a Divine light he often read the secrets of hearts. Even when at a distance from his Superiors he was oftentimes acquainted with their unspoken thoughts, whenever these had any reference to his own conduct. This marvellous gift was repeatedly manifested during the course of his life. It was first discovered by his Rector, Father Fiocchi, in the fol-lowing manner: He had sent the wonderful Brother with a document to Lacedogna. Gerard had al-ready proceeded some distance on his way, when

Father Fiocchi remembered that he had forgotten something of importance in his letter.

"What a pity," he said to himself, "that I cannot bring Brother Gerard back."

This expression of his Superior's will, purely mental though it was, sufficed for our Saint. Almighty God was pleased mysteriously to reveal it to His servant, who at once retraced his steps. On his return to the house Father Fiocchi asked him in surprise what had made him come back so soon. Saint Gerard said nothing, but only smiled, thus causing the Rector to understand that he was there in obedience to his secret wish.

Henceforth, whenever Father Fiocchi desired to give Gerard an order, if he was not with him at the time, he gave the command silently in his own mind. This was enough. He was always obeyed as though he had spoken aloud.

On one occasion the Father Rector was conversing at Melfi with the Bishop of the diocese on the life of extraordinary sanctity that was led by Saint Gerard. The Bishop had heard of the holy Brother, and for some time had been desirous of forming his acquaintance. He now said that he would gladly send a special messenger to bring him to the Palace.

"That will not be necessary," said Father Fiocchi; "I have but to tell him mentally to come, and he will soon be here. Your Lordship will thus see how far his obedience reaches, and how specially he is favoured by Almighty God."

At the same moment in the Convent, far away at home, Gerard understood of a sudden that his Father Rector desired his presence. Accordingly, having obtained the necessary permission, and given his reasons for going to the Father in charge of the House, he set off for Melfi. On arriving at the Episcopal Palace, he found the Father Rector with the Bishop. Father Fiocchi pretended to be displeased at his coming, and asked him stiffly what brought him there.

"It was your Reverence's wish," simply answered Gerard.

"What!" exclaimed Father Fiocchi, "my wish! I never wrote to you, and I sent you no messenger."

"Nevertheless," was the reply, " nevertheless your Reverence was pleased to give me a formal obedience to come to you. The Bishop wishes to speak with me. Alas! who am I that anyone should wish to speak with me I I am only a worm of the earth, a sinner, a poor wretch who have the greatest need of all the mercy of God."

Under normal circumstances a Redemptorist Lay-brother hardly ever sleeps outside his convent walls, excepting in those countries where a Brother accompanies the Fathers to do the domestic work of the house in which they may be lodging during the time of Mission. Saint Gerard, however, was to be an exception to the ordinary rule.

God had called him to the heights of contemplation, and infused into his soul the most sublime lights on the deepest mysteries of our holy religion. He was endowed with the spirit of prophecy. The future was often unrolled as an open scroll before his eyes. Nothing, however seemingly impossible, was refused his prayer. He worked miracles of healing almost as easily – with as little effect – as others discharge the ordinary functions of life. All these gratuitous gifts of God were not designed to be hidden in a napkin. They had been bestowed upon him more for the sake of others than for his own. He was to be as a beacon-light, proclaiming to the tempest-tossed mariner, cast on the billows of life's angry ocean, the closeness of God, in the midst of the storm – the nearness of the unseen haven of everlasting rest.

Thus Divine Providence arranged that for the remainder of his life Saint Gerard should be much in the busy haunts of men. The house at Iliceto was in such poverty that it became absolutely necessary, unless either the Foundation was to be abandoned altogether, or the community be exposed to the danger of dying of starvation, that an appeal should be made for outside help.

In this emergency, Gerard was sent out by his Superiors to "quest," that is, to solicit alms for the support of his Convent. Everywhere he was received by the people with open arms. All had the warmest of welcomes for him wherever he went. It was felt that when Gerard visited a house, there came by his side a blessing to abide where he had rested, as a gracious Presence – even after his bodily departure – the blessing of the peace of God which he brought, to remain with faithful souls who responded to his appeals, in the Name and for the Love of Jesus Christ.

Indeed, his coming excited such enthusiasm among the warm-hearted people of southern Italy, that the only difficulty was to restrain their generosity within due bounds. Ladies wished to give him their earrings. Men, who had nothing else, desired to cut the very buttons – often so valuable in Italy – off their clothes that they might give unto the Lord and His servant that which cost them something. As he passed along his way, people knelt to receive his benediction, and cried out to one another:

"The Saint – the Saint is coming! Here is the Saint!"

Still Brother Gerard's humility remained as profound as ever. Unmoved by the applause of men, he reposed all his confidence in God alone. No breath of pride was suffered to dim the lustre of his virtue – no uprising of self-complacency permitted to cloud the serenity of his childlike spirit. Through the light that he received from above, his own nothingness was never absent from his sight. Considering the abundance of the Divine gifts which had been lavished so freely upon his soul, he marvelled at what he deemed his base ingratitude. Like Saint Francis of Assisi, he looked upon himself as the last and least of men, and found his peace in his own abjection.

He hath put down the powerful from their seat, and hath exalted the lowly and the meek. He hath filled the hungry with good things, and the rich He hath sent empty away.

HIS JOURNEYINGS TO AND FRO

A few years after the holy death of Saint Gerard, a Lay-brother belonging to some Mendicant Order, was out "questing" for his Convent. While going his rounds one day in the company of two Priests of the locality, he entered the house of an old lady who was nearly blind. When she asked who her visitors might be, and what was the object of their visit, one of the Priests replied that it was a Brother come to beg an alms for the support of his Monastery. Whereupon the good old lady got up at once, and walked as quickly as she could across the room, saying:

"O my dear Brother Gerard, let me, I beg of you, kiss your hand!"

The astonished Brother had now of course to explain matters. It was a case of mistaken identity. Brother Gerard had died some time previously.

"Brother Gerard dead! Brother Gerard dead!" cried out the old lady in dismay. "Oh! he was indeed a great Saint."

She then related how the holy servant of God had once visited her house in a time of general dearth. For her comfort he had foretold that she would be able with the one bushel of meal, which yet remained in her store, to provide for all the wants of her family until the next harvest. Everything happened exactly as he had promised. Contrary to the laws of human possibility, this meal held out with but little visible diminution until the season of plenty arrived. Once more it was made manifest that what is impossible with men, is possible with God. Indeed, not only did it amply suffice for the needs of the whole family and of several workmen as well, but there even remained some over and above after all their wants had been provided for. This the mistress of the house remembered that she had been able to sell. She now gladly and gratefully gave the Brother a liberal alms in memory of the Saint, who had been her great benefactor.

If the mere recollection of Gerard thus provoked charity after his death, we may easily imagine his influence during life. Wherever he went he won the affection and confidence of the people by the kindness of his heart and his wonderful miracles, while at the same time he often gained the greatest sinners for God by disclosing, to their amazement, secrets of the past which they believed known to no mortal man.

Not long after his Profession he returned to his native city of Muro, there to collect alms for his Convent. At Muro he stayed with one Alexander Piccolo, a watchmaker by trade. The son of this man one day fell down in the street in a fit. He was stunned by his fall, and carried into a neighbouring house in a state of unconsciousness. The people thought that he was dying. Loud were the cries of grief that rent the air. As soon, however, as Saint

Gerard appeared upon the scene, all was changed. Quietly saying that it would be nothing, he knelt down and made the sign of the Cross upon the boy's forehead, who that instant was seen to rise without delay or difficulty from the ground restored to a perfect state of health and strength, amidst loud exclamations of grateful wonderment from the crowd, which had gradually gathered round.

When looked at in the light of Faith, far more wonderful than any bodily cure is the conversion of a soul to God. There was in Muro a notary, named Peter de Rubertis, who had been guilty of a homicide which was known to God alone. He had in his orchard a specially fine cherry-tree. The better to guard his property, he used to keep watch over it himself. Now one evening, coming upon a thief in his garden, he let him off with threats as to the consequences should he be found marauding a second time. However, he soon caught the same man again. Once more he restrained his anger. But when, emboldened by impunity, the thief returned anew, it was too much for de Rubertis to bear. In his fury – whether more or less accidentally or deliberately is not clear – he assaulted him with fatal results, and then buried the dead body in the orchard. As this tragedy occurred during the night, the missing man was never traced, and his murderer was not brought to justice. He kept his dread secret locked up in the inmost recesses of his own breast. From God he could not hide it, but he was mad enough to conceal it from the Priest of God even in the sacred tribunal of penance. For years he had made bad Confessions, and lived in a terrible state of sacrilege, until God, in His great mercy, brought him one day into contact with Saint Gerard. The holy Brother looked at the poor man intently, and then said to him without more ado:

"Sir, your conscience is indeed in a sad state. You will have to make your Confessions all over again, beginning from the time when you killed that man near the cherry-tree, and then buried him in your orchard. You have never told it yet in Confession."

The guilty man was thunderstruck. On his return home he told all to his wife, who made the whole story known after his death. Meanwhile his soul had been won by the Saint. He hastened to approach the Sacraments in good earnest. No longer was he a sacrilegious trifler with holy things. A real penitent, he hastened to make a good Confession, and thus regained the peace of mind that had not been his for many a year, and which in all probability never would have been his again, had it not been for Brother Gerard's charity.

For three years the servant of God was passing and repassing through the kingdom of Naples on his appointed rounds, everywhere persuading the greatest sinners to turn away from vice and lead a life of virtue. We cannot here do more than select two or three of the tales of wonder that embellish the story of these journeys with a beauty all their own. Saint Gerard was deeply steeped in the true Franciscan spirit, and we find him, like Saint Francis and Saint Antony, often calling to his aid the services of his "brothers the animals," who, whenever there was question of causing sin to be avoided, or of teaching some deep spiritual truth, seemed almost to be endowed for the moment with the gift of reason at his word.

On one occasion he noticed that the horse he was riding – for Gerard's journeys, according to the custom of the time, were usually made on horseback – had lost its shoes. So he went to the nearest forge and asked to have the beast re-shod. His task performed, the blacksmith claimed an exorbitant sum in payment. Now Gerard had made a Vow of Poverty. The money that was demanded of him was not his to give. Besides, he wished to teach the man a wholesome lesson. So he deliberately told the horse to take the shoes off again, that there might be nothing for which to pay. The animal stepped forward, shook its hoofs, and lo! the shoes fell to the earth. The blacksmith was struck mute with astonishment. But after a few moments, as he saw the figure of Saint Gerard riding away on his unshod steed and gradually disappearing in the distance, he called out loudly:

"Gerard, Gerard, will you come back for one instant?"

Brother Gerard, however, was not thus to be brought back, He proceeded quietly on his journey.

The servant of God had but to call the little birds, and they would come flocking round him and perch on his hand. We are told that the young nephew of a certain priest, Don Salvatore by name, had a bird given to him which he kept in a cage in his room. Gerard, pitying it in its unnatural captivity, opened the cage and let it fly happily away. But as the child began to cry bitterly at the loss of his pet, Gerard went to the window, and called out:

"Come back, little bird, come back, the child is crying. He wants you."

Back came the little creature, obedient to the voice of Gerard, who restored it to its owner.

On another occasion, when on his way to Corato, the Saint met a small farmer who was in great distress. The field-mice were destroying all the produce of his land, on which he was absolutely dependent for the support of his family. Saint Gerard's tender heart was filled with compassion for the sad condition of these poor people. Accordingly, he asked the farmer whether he would prefer the mice to die, or would he have them go elsewhere?

"Let them all die," was the decisive answer that came without a moment's hesitation.

"Very well!" assented Gerard.

He then raised his hand, and made the sign of the Cross in the direction of the field. That same instant its surface was strewn with dead and dying mice. Amazed at the wonderful sight that met his view, our farmer, beside himself with delight, went full haste into Corato, spreading the news far and wide that a great Saint would soon be in the town.

We will now relate a miracle of another kind. The holy Brother once went into a strange house and asked for something to eat. He begged it, he said, as an alms for the love of God. The poor woman to whom this appeal was made had not so much as a morsel of bread in the house. Like the widow of whom we read in the Scripture story, she had only a handful of flour. This she had just brought home from the mill. So she told Saint Gerard that having nothing for herself, she had nothing to give away.

"What! You have nothing, and that bin is all full of bread!"

"It is empty," persisted the woman. "I have not so much as a piece of bread in the whole house."

Gerard, however, persuaded her just to raise the lid of the bin. There was no room for doubt about the matter. It was indeed full of most excellent bread!

We will conclude this chapter with the quaint account that has been handed down to us of a famous conversion effected by our Saint. He was going home to Iliceto, after having been for some time absent, collecting alms in the neighbourhood. His cloak was patched; his habit old and short; his hat was a marvel of poverty. Altogether, the appearance he presented seemed sufficiently weird to a young man whom he chanced to fall in with on the road. The thought suddenly flashed across his mind that Gerard could be no other than a wandering gipsy. Dreaming of little save the acquisition of gold and silver, it also occurred to him that he had met an adept in Occult Science who was searching for a hidden treasure.

"Oh! if I could only share his secret," he thought within himself, "then perchance I might also share his treasure."

Straightway he accosted Gerard.

"Perhaps, sir," he asked bluntly, "perhaps you are a wizard?"

"Perhaps I am! Perhaps I am not!" was Gerard's reply.

Confirmed in his singular misunderstanding by this evasive answer, the young man now boldly made his request.

"If you are searching for a treasure," he said, "I

am most ready to help you. Let me offer you my services."

"But," questioned Gerard, "are you a man of mind and a man of courage to boot?"

"Little do you guess all that I am," answered the stranger eagerly, and then followed the sad tale of a life of sin, with the final avowal that it was full six years since the unhappy being had last approached the Sacraments.

"Well, well," chimed in Gerard, "you then, without a doubt, are the very man for whom I will now most gladly seek a treasure. Only do as I bid you, and the treasure is yours."

So together they walked, deep in conversation, until at last they reached a forest thick with brushwood. Gerard was the first to enter. His companion, full of suppressed excitement, thought that now his desires were on the very point of being realized. When at last they were in the midst of a tangled copse, the Brother took off his cloak, slowly and mysteriously laid it on the ground, and then beckoned to his new friend to advance. The young man began to quake and tremble with fear. Every shadow cast by the trees seemed to be a living form; every moment he expected to behold an apparition of the Prince of Darkness. Gerard saw that his opportunity had arrived. Suddenly he took out his crucifix, and holding it up before the eyes of the astonished lad, said gently:

"Yes! I promised you a Treasure. Behold it here! The Treasure of all treasures. The Treasure which you have so madly bartered for the wages of sin."

The hour of grace had struck. The poor boy was touched to the quick. He burst forth into bitter sobs. Gerard, seeing him thus pierced with sorrow for having offended Our Blessed Lord, pressed him lovingly to his heart. He then brought him home to the Convent, where he kept him several days, and induced him to make his peace with God by a good Confession of the evil past.

Truly a wizard indeed!

MONTE GARGANO

One Easter holidays, the Redemptorist Students, who were studying Theology at Iliceto under the care of the celebrated Father de Meo, conceived a great desire to visit the holy grotto of Monte Gargano. Monte Gargano is the well-known shrine which the glorious Saint Michael had long ages before miraculously pointed out as the chosen spot where it was the Divine Will that special honour should be paid to him and to all the angelic choirs of Heaven.

The Father Rector acceded to the request that was made to him to authorize a pilgrimage to this favoured mountain, and directed that Saint Gerard should be responsible for all the arrangements and be the guide of the whole party. Father Fiocchi remembered the life-long devotion of our Saint to the great Archangel. Indeed, the holy Brother's heart was full to overflowing at the thought of being thus permitted to pay public homage to one to whose loving care he had been so marvellously indebted in the days of his childhood for his first Communion.

This famous expedition to Monte Gargano was

an unbroken chain of prodigies and graces. The pilgrims numbered twelve in all – ten students, Father de Meo, and Saint Gerard. The journey there and back could not at that time be accomplished in less than a week. To provide for all their temporal necessities, they had the magnificent sum of twelve shillings – exactly a shilling a-piece! But there were giants on earth in those days. The Community at Iliceto was poor in this world's goods, but rich in the possession of a great Saint among its members. Superiors relied with confidence on the prudence and charity of Saint Gerard – above all, on his power with God. The event proved that they were not resting on a broken reed.

When, before starting, the students, in blank dismay, remonstrated with their appointed leader on the slenderness of their resources, he only smiled and said:

"God will provide."

This is ever the motto of the Saints. To their unfailing confidence in the good Providence of our heavenly Father, they owe the wonderful answers to their prayers. It is Faith that moves mountains. If we believed and trusted like the Saints, like the Saints also we should be heard on high and become omnipotent with God.

The first halt made by the little band was at Foggia. Here it was that Saint Alphonsus, while preaching to a crowded congregation, had on two separate occasions been rapt in ecstasy before a miraculous picture of the Blessed Virgin, surrounded by rays of light that darted towards him from Our Lady's countenance, and supernaturally raised in the air. These extraordinary facts had been witnessed by hundreds, and were public prop-

erty at the time. We may then without much difficulty realize the devotion with which the young
Redemptorists would pay their filial homage to the
great Mother of God at the very shrine where she
had bestowed on the holy Founder of their Insti-
tute such marked proofs of her maternal love.

During their short stay at Foggia, a nun in the
Convent of the Annunciation expressed the wish to
speak with Saint Gerard on the concerns of her
soul. Great was her surprise when the holy Brother
told her that she would soon be called upon to appear before the Judgment Seat of God. She was
quite young, and in perfect health. However, in
four months she was no more.

At the commencement of the pilgrimage, the
luggage had been placed on two asses and con-
signed to the care of a hermit of the locality who
accompanied the expedition. But after the first
night, Gerard, seeing that the young students were
quite tired out by the long walking of the previous
day, and listening only to the dictates of his kindly
heart, determined to hire a carriage.

"How are we to pay for it?" asked they.

"God will provide," was the Brother's only
answer.

Accordingly, he engaged a carriage and pair
for the company. The unfortunate donkeys
dragged laboriously behind, as best they might,
under the charge of their conductor. When they
stopped at their first halting-place, in order to take
some refreshments, they had to wait long hours for
the luggage and the hermit. At last the poor man
arrived, all breathless and covered with dust.
Gerard made him take the nourishment that he
evidently so badly needed, and then gave the signal

for a fresh start. But at this our hermit proved re-
fractory. He said that his beasts would fall dead by
the road-side. They should not move another inch
that day.

"They are not going to remain here," said Gerard, "I will see to it all."

The hermit had no choice but to surrender at
discretion. Notwithstanding his repugnance to
travel farther, he mounted one of the asses, while
Gerard made the son of the owner of the carriage
get up on the other. The donkeys thus mounted
were then, by the orders of the Saint, brought to
the front of the vehicle, while he himself took his
position on the box-seat, and giving the two asses a
flick with his whip, said aloud:

"In the name of the Most Holy Trinity I command you to take the lead."

A moment before, the beasts were utterly exhausted, but now a new strength comes to them.
They go briskly on their way, galloping when the
carriage-horses gallop, walking when they walk,
giving no more trouble to anyone! Thus all went
well until they reached the next stage of the journey, a place called Manfredonia.

Here it became necessary to pay for the carriage. When the bill had been paid, there remained
but a few pence in the purse. Nothing daunted,
however, at this somewhat critical state of affairs,
when Gerard saw some pretty bouquets of flowers,
that were exposed for sale in the market-place, he
bought one in order to place it before Our Lord in
the Blessed Sacrament. He then went straight to
the church, mounted the steps of the Altar, laid the
bouquet before the tabernacle, knelt down and said
simply:

"O Lord, Thou dost see that I have thought of Thee. It now remains for Thee to think of me."

It happened that at that moment the chaplain in charge entered the church. He saw and heard all. Thinking within himself that this must be some great servant of God, he went up to him, and offered him the hospitality of his house.

"May God reward you," said Gerard, "but we are a large party."

"Never mind that," was the reply, "you are all most welcome. You will, I am sure, accept the indifferent hospitality that it is in my power to offer you. Unfortunately, my poor mother has been ill for the past two months. She will therefore be unable to attend to your wants as she would have wished."

"That can be remedied easily enough," was Gerard's quick answer. "All you have to do is to go back to the house, make the sign of the Cross on the forehead of your mother, and she will, believe me, be immediately cured."

Faith begets faith. The chaplain did as he was bid, and his mother was well at once. Thus do the Saints repay the favours that are shown them!

The chaplain on his side was not ungrateful for grace that he had received. He made Gerard an offering of money to help towards the expenses of the rest of the journey, and sent the pilgrims with a God-speed on their road.

At last they reached Monte Gargano. Here they joyfully satisfied their devotion to the great Archangel, but at last, tired out as they were from the ascent of the holy mountain, nature craved for rest and refreshment. Where was Gerard? No one had seen him for some time. At last they found him

rapt in an ecstasy, his face turned up towards
Heaven, his eyes fixed as though gazing silently on
some object unseen to all save himself alone, his
body motionless as a statue. For some time it was
impossible to rouse him. At last he slowly came to
himself, as if awakening from a deep slumber. On
seeing himself surrounded by his companions, his
humility was disturbed. Covered with confusion, he
said quickly:

"It is nothing. It is nothing. Let us now think of
getting something to eat."

Thus did he tear himself from the Divine Embraces, to provide even for the bodily needs of others. That night they passed in an inn close to the
holy grotto. The morning was consecrated to devotion. But next day there came a new difficulty.
Once more their funds were at a low ebb. The
money so generously given them by the kind chaplain was all but exhausted. How were they to get
another dinner? Gerard told them all to sit down
without more ado, for God would surely provide.
In a few moments – it was a day of abstinence- the
table was covered with several dishes of excellent
fish. Where could the fish have come from? Great
was the excitement to find out. Gerard held his
peace. The hermit who did their commission was
then questioned on the subject. He said in reply
that the previous night the Saint, on perceiving
that he had almost come to the end of his resources, had knelt in prayer before the Altar of the
Archangel, when suddenly a stranger came up to
him, and placed a roll of money in his hands, with
the words:

"Take that, pray for me, and do you love God
more and more."

It was now time to think of returning. When they asked for the account, the innkeeper sent in an exorbitant charge. This Gerard was not going to pay. He said quietly:

"Unless you are satisfied with what is really due to you, you will lose all your mules."

That very moment in rushed mine host's son.

"Come, father, come quickly!" he cried; "I cannot understand what has happened to the mules. They are rolling about the ground in a frightful way – come quickly!"

The man then knew that he had to deal with a Saint. Terror-stricken, he cast himself at the feet of the Servant of God, imploring his pardon.

"I pardon you gladly," said Gerard, "but never forget that God takes the side of His poor. It will go badly with you if you ever attempt to defraud them again."

Saint Gerard then insisted on paying the amount which was really due, and left the house. Before departing from the spot, he made the sign of the Cross over the poor mules. They immediately gave every sign of the possession of their pristine vigour.

At the foot of the mountain, the young students complained that they were consumed by a parching thirst.

"Patience!" cried Gerard, "there is, remember, a well a little farther on."

But on their arrival at the eagerly expected spot they were dismayed to find that the rope by which the bucket was lowered had been removed. They could gaze, but only gaze, upon the tantalizing sight of the cool water as it sparkled temptingly below them far beyond their reach. The owner of the place had taken advantage of the prevailing drought to extort payment from the thirsty traveller, even for that which God gives freely to all His children. Saint Gerard besought this avaricious man not to be so hard-hearted as to refuse the poor pilgrims the means of slaking their thirst. All, however, was in vain. Gerard pressed his case again and again, only to meet with reiterated refusals. At last the Servant of God pleaded no longer.

"Since," he said, in a tone of menace, "you refuse even a cup of water to your neighbour, whom you are bound to love as you love yourself, soon the well in its turn will refuse to supply your wants."

With these words Gerard turned away, but scarcely was he gone before the wretched man came running after him, begging him for God's sake to return and not delay. It was, he bewailed, the only well in all that neighbourhood. What would happen to him? What would happen to the country-side? Even while Gerard was still speaking, it appeared that the water had commenced gradually to subside, obedient to his voice, and now the well was completely empty. Hence the consternation of its owner.

"Come back, come back, all of you, I entreat you!" he exclaimed; "you shall have plenty to drink, you and your beasts as well."

Gerard's companions, accustomed though they were to his miracles, could hardly believe their ears. Quickly they retraced their steps, and, leaning over the kerb of the well, beheld with wonder dry stones where, a few minutes before, the water had been glistening in the sun. They then turned to the Saint, and begged him further to exercise his power and give them something wherewith to assuage their burning thirst. Straightway the water was seen to reappear, bubbling slowly upwards, and not stopping until the well was as full as before the catastrophe.

"I beg of you," said Gerard, as a final word of friendly warning to the proprietor who, true to his word, now hastened to supply the pilgrims' needs – "I beg of you never more to refuse to anyone that which belongs of right to all the world. If you do, you will find to your cost that God will again refuse it to yourself."

They then all quenched their thirst, and we are told that, from that day forward, the offence was never repeated. Water was never refused from that well to any who passed by – at least during the lifetime of him to whom Saint Gerard had taught the duty of charity by a sermon more eloquent than could be preached from any pulpit.

On their way home the pilgrims visited not only Our Lady of Foggia once more, but also a little chapel in a sequestered wood dedicated to Maria Coronata. Here Saint Gerard went into yet another ecstasy. His companions must have been well used to the sight by this time. Yet one of them ventured to ask him, when he came to himself, what had been the matter with him during the trance.

"Oh! it is nothing," was the humble answer, "it is only a weakness to which I am subject."

Thus ended the famous pilgrimage to Monte Gargano, a pilgrimage never to be forgotten by those who took part in it. Among these was a young man called Peter Paul Blasucci, brother to the young novice, Dominic Blasucci, whose life has been written by Saint Alphonsus, and who had died in the freshness of his first fervour, and in the odour of great sanctity a few months previously. Peter Paul Blasucci at this time was barely a year professed. But during this journey, Saint Gerard told him that one day he would be elected Superior-General of the Congregation of the Most Holy Redeemer. The prophecy was fulfilled forty years later, when, in the year 1793, the General Chapter elected Father Blasucci to govern the Congregation founded by Saint Alphonsus.

The pilgrimage to Monte Gargano had lasted nine days. The little band returned with their purse better replenished than when they first started on their pious travels.

Confidence in Divine Providence is a bank that never breaks, a well that never runs dry.

HIS VISITS TO THE WORLD

The supernatural gifts of Saint Gerard and his great reputation for sanctity caused frequent applications to be addressed to his Superiors that he might be permitted from time to time to visit friends of the Congregation in various towns of the locality. Such visits are, as we have already observed, contrary to all custom. But every law has its necessary exceptions. Thus in this case, after great difficulties had at first been raised, the desired permission at length was freely given. On the one hand, the position of the applicants in many instances was such that it would have been hard always to refuse them; on the other hand, even the strictest Superior might well shrink from the responsibility of keeping Brother Gerard within convent walls, when the good of souls outside seemed to cry aloud for his presence in their midst.

Indeed, it is not too much to say that Gerard sanctified every spot which he visited. His coming was like a Mission for the people. The house that was privileged to receive him as its guest was daily besieged by persons drawn from all classes of society. Crowds might be observed at all hours gathered round about him, and hanging eagerly on the words that fell from his lips. Such, as we may again and again observe in the annals of the Church's story, is the mysterious, magnetic attraction of the Saints of God upon the souls of men.

Strange as it may sound, not only lay-people, but Priests and even Bishops vied one with another in their anxiety to obtain the advice of this lowly Lay-brother. Saint Gerard was frequently consulted both on the personal perplexities of individual consciences, and also on abstruse questions of dogmatic theology. Advice, wise, clear, and always most practical, he refused to none who sought his aid. On the most sublime mysteries of our holy religion he spoke as one inspired, for he was in truth a man full of faith and of the Holy Ghost. He had also received that which is known as the gift of "infused knowledge" in abundant measure.

Those who listened to the burning words of this poor Brother, uneducated in secular learning, but so deeply versed in the wisdom that comes from Heaven, could only praise God Who had hidden His Divine secrets from the wise and prudent to make them known to the pure and simple of heart. That Gerard was a great Saint could be doubted by none who were conversant with his unearthly ways and heavenly endowments. He appeared to live in an atmosphere of marvel. The very air he breathed seemed redolent of the supernatural. Strong men would tremble, awe-stricken at the nearness of the all-knowing Spirit of God, as Gerard read the inmost recesses of their hearts. Ofttimes it was known by the result that the future had been even as the present to his illumined gaze. To work miracles through love for his fellow-crea-

tures, out of heartfelt compassion for them in their
various trials and afflictions, was as his daily bread.

Yet it was not this rich accumulation of Divine
gifts that struck the imagination of men or appealed to their highest and noblest feelings so
forcibly, as the spectacle of the Christ-like virtues in
recompense for which those gifts were given. An
emissary of Satan can disguise himself as an Angel
of Light, and may even counterfeit the miracles of
the Saints; but humility, sweetness, voluntary
poverty, charity, peace – these are unmistakable in
their origin, and these, exercised in an heroic degree, were conspicuously the graces that adorned
the beautiful soul of Gerard. Dear to God and
dear to man, none could resist his gentle sway, and
great were the conversions that he worked for Jesus
Christ his Master.

Corato, his native city of Muro, Castelgrande,
Melfi, are the names of the places where his stay
would seem to have been productive of the most
permanent results. These little towns, according to
trustworthy testimony, were altogether changed by
his presence in their midst.

God was pleased to show by a manifest sign on
his first entrance to Corato that He was with His
servant Gerard. It had been arranged by his Superiors that he was to stay in the house of a gentleman named Papaleo. As the Saint had never
been to Corato before, he had no idea where his
host lived. So he let the bridle fall loosely on his
horse's neck, and abandoned himself into the
hands of Divine Providence. The faithful animal
went on quietly until it came to the house of Papaleo, when it entered the courtyard.

"Can you tell me where Don Papaleo lives?"

asked Gerard, on seeing that they had come to a
standstill.

"Why, Brother, here you are!" was the answer
he received. The Saint then dismounted, thanking
God the while.

He was summoned to Castelgrande in order to
put an end to a terrible feud which was the scandal
of the town. Some years previously a young man
had been killed in a quarrel. His parents cherished
a hatred, dark and deadly, towards him whom they
regarded as the murderer of their son. After two
interviews, Gerard at length succeeded in persuading the poor father to sacrifice his desire of
revenge, and even to promise that he would be
publicly reconciled with the man who was guilty of
his son's death.

Meanwhile, full of gratitude to God for his suc-
cess, Gerard was called away on other business to
Muro. What, then, must have been his pain and
dismay on returning after a few days to discover
that in his absence all his work had been completely undone. To all appearance once more it
was useless to interfere. All prospect of reconciliation had seemingly vanished into the grave of
buried hopes. Matters were even more serious than
they had been before his first arrival on the scene.

The man's wife, infuriated at the news that her
husband had promised to forgive the enemy of his
house, had brought him the blood-stained gar-
ments of their dead child, which she had always
carefully preserved. Then, in a terrible paroxysm
of mingled grief and rage, she had appealed to the
unhappy father – by all the memories which that
sight recalled – was he going to be so base as to
make friends with the murderer of their poor boy?

Yes, she continued, well might he gaze at that blood. Still did it cry aloud to Heaven for vengeance – a vengeance upon which, alas! it had not yet been hers to feast her eyes. Pardon such a wretch! Never, to her dying day!

These wild and wicked words had their effect. To his grief, Gerard recognized the fact that the last state of that man in the sight of God was far worse than his first. He had steeled himself sternly against every appeal that could be made. It seemed quite useless to speak to him. Forgive he would not. His anger was implacable.

Still the Saint was not to be refused. He knelt down before the injured parents, laid his Crucifix on the ground by his side, and asked them were they prepared to trample on their Saviour's Wounds. This they do who will not forgive. All, however, was as yet in vain. Their hearts were touched indeed, but not conquered until the Servant of God struck another chord. Would they not make this sacrifice for the sake of the son they loved so well? Let them offer it up in suffrage for the relief of his poor soul. God, he promised them – it had been revealed to him from above – would most surely accept such an offering. Let them freely forgive the murderer, and then have five Masses offered for their dear child – this would suffice in satisfaction for the debt he still owed the Justice of God for his past sins. By closing their hearts to the claims of mercy and Christian forgiveness, they-his parents – were at the same time taking out of their own hands the power to help the poor boy who – Gerard knew it – was even then in Purgatory.

This was enough. Now at length the victory

was won. The father and mother could resist no longer. They generously performed everything that was asked of them. A reconciliation was happily effected between the family of the murdered man and that of the murderer, complete forgiveness extended by the injured ones to him who had so cruelly wronged them, and both families ever afterwards united together in the bonds of Christian friendship, to the edification of the whole locality. We may add that this great miracle of grace – for such it might rightly be called – was, in God's Providence, worked by the Holy Spirit to the glory of Saint Gerard at Castelgrande, the very place where in youth he had permitted himself, out of love for the despised Jesus, to be mocked by the boys as a fool in the public streets.

To return to Gerard's flying visit to Muro. Our Lord had made use of His servant's visit to that city to secure the salvation of another soul that was in the most imminent danger of perishing everlastingly. There lived in Muro at the time a woman called Catherine Zaccardi, the wife of a jeweller of the place. She had been for several years at enmity with God. Gerard had more than once stayed in her house on previous occasions, but had never until now spoken to her on the sad state of her soul. Indeed, her sins were known only to herself and to the great Searcher of hearts. During this visit, however, the Saint had a special revelation concerning her secret sins and approaching death. He did not hesitate a moment. Taking his hostess aside, he entreated her with all earnestness to make a good Confession without delay, and thus prepare to meet her Sovereign Judge, for her days on earth were numbered. He bade her remember that, un-

less she laid bare to the Physician of her soul the
sins that until then were hidden in the recesses of
her guilty conscience, she must lose the sight of
God for all eternity. Catherine enjoyed perfect
health when God in His Goodness sent her this
solemn warning. Shortly afterwards, however, she
was attacked by a dangerous malady. In a few
months she was dead.

Saint Gerard had paid several visits to Melfi,
and was already well known in that place, when in
the year 1753 the Bishop asked Father Fiocchi to
preach a public Novena in the Cathedral. He requested also, as a special favour, that the holy
Brother might accompany his Rector, and remain
with him while the spiritual exercises lasted.

Numerous are the accounts that have been left
to posterity of the wonderful conversions operated
by Saint Gerard at Melfi. At the wish of the
Bishop, any particularly hardened sinners were en-
trusted to the care of the Servant of God. He
spoke to them so winningly and so wisely as at
once to change the most hardened hearts. God was
with him, and no one could resist the power that
spoke by his lips. He then conducted his prisoners
of love to Father Fiocchi, who gladly heard their
Confessions, and reconciled them with Our Lord.
He likewise rescued several secret sinners from the
snares of Satan through the supernatural light by
which he was able to read even in the inmost
depths of the soul.

In the year 1843, ninety years after the visit to
Melfi, a very old man, now nearly a hundred years
of age, was able to give the following testimony
before the commission appointed to take evidence
with a view to Brother Gerard's Beatification:

"I was a mere child," he deposed, "when Gerard came to Melfi. To the young people, who used to flock around him, he was accustomed always to dwell on the love of God, at the same time urging them to fidelity in the performance of their religious duties. He would usually finish his little discourses by some such words as these: 'We understand one another, then, do we not? We are going to give ourselves up altogether to the good God.' He then signed our foreheads with the sign of the Cross, and gave us little pictures of Our Lady of Seven Dolours. He was most mortified. . . . Charitable and kind towards the poor, he was wont to rob himself of food in order to be able to give to the needy. Once I saw him deprive himself even of his shoes and stockings to hand them over to a beggar. But that which was most remarkable in him was his zeal for the conversion of sinners."

The conversion of sinners. Of a truth this was the one consuming passion of Saint Gerard's heart.

HIS CHARITY DURING AN EPIDEMIC

P erhaps there was no spot in all Southern Italy where Gerard was better known or held in higher esteem than in the little town of Lacedogna. Here for three long years he had served the hard master whose violent temper had so exercised him in the practice of virtue. Here he had lived, in the sight of men and angels, a life of heroic sanctity, even before his entrance into Religion. Here was "Gerard's Well," recalling by its very name the great Miracle of the Bambino, worked in reward of Gerard's faith.

Whenever, therefore, the Servant of God had occasion to visit Lacedogna, he was received with open arms by its inhabitants. And now the little city was in sore distress. A terrible pestilence had invaded its streets. Panic and dismay reigned supreme, while not a few recognized in the visitation which had come upon them so suddenly, the Divine punishment for notorious scandals that existed in their midst. There was a general demand for Gerard. He, it was felt, could stay the anger of God.

The Bishop of the place accordingly represented his own desire and that of his people for the visit from the holy Brother, with the result that the Saint was sent by his Superiors to Lacedogna. Saint Gerard took up his abode with an excellent Christian called Constantine Capucci. This good man and his family were filled with enthusiasm at the sight of the virtues of their guest; especially were they moved by the austerity of life which nothing could hide, and by his exceeding charity.

Every day great numbers of persons, Priests and laymen, flocked to Capucci's house in order to seek the advice of his holy visitor. Ever full of affability, he was accessible to all. No time was kept by him as his own. His one desire was to be of service to his fellow-men. Nor were signs and wonders absent. God glorified His servant before the world, that hearts might be the more docile in his hands.

On one occasion Gerard was with his host and a large number of friends in the picture gallery of the house. Suddenly he went into an ecstasy, and was transported off his feet to the level of a picture of the Holy Mother of God that was hanging upon the walls. Then remaining for some time supernaturally raised in the air, beside himself with love, he cried aloud:

"How beautiful she is! How beautiful! How beautiful is Mary!"

As he spoke, he covered the picture with rapturous kisses. We may easily imagine the holy confusion he must have experienced when, on coming to himself, he discovered to his dismay that quite a large assemblage had thus become witnesses of the Divine favours of which he was the recipient.

The first person to be cured at Lacedogna was a Priest, Canon Saponiero. He had received the last Sacraments, and was given over by the doctors, when Saint Gerard brought him back from the very jaws of death. This worthy Canon has himself left us an account of his cure. After describing the complicated nature of his maladies, he proceeds as follows:

"I thought myself on the point of appearing before the Judgment-Seat of God. Having heard of the arrival of the holy Brother, I had myself recommended to his powerful prayers. What was not my amazement when he sent me word that my illness would not be of long duration, and that all I needed for recovery was complete confidence in God. I might then still hope, and when he visited me the next day, I cried out, 'Praised be the Lord!' He answered me, 'Rejoice, you are cured.' Then he came close up to me, and made on my forehead the sign of the Cross. At once I found myself perfectly well. I should have risen that moment, had he not enjoined upon me to wait for the morrow. Glory be to God, and to His servant!"

By the sign of the Holy Cross he cured many other persons. Thus he succeeded in restoring to her former state of health a young girl called Leila Cocchia, who for some months previously had been the victim of a terrible form of madness.

Saint Gerard knew Leila of old. On one of his former visits to Lacedogna she had come to him, inconsolable with grief, and asked him about the soul of her mother, for whose recent death she was then mourning. The Saint had received a Divine light, by which he was able to tell her that her mother was in Purgatory, but that she would be delivered if her daughter would offer forty Communions for her eternal repose. She did as she was asked, and after making the Communions, her mother appeared to her, thanked her, and told her that she was on her way to Heaven.

Gerard remembered all this, and was grieved indeed to hear of the poor girl's afflicted state. He went straight to her house. On his arrival, according to his usual custom, he made the sign of the Cross, and at once she recovered the use of her reason. The recovery was both complete and permanent.

Such favours as these, published as they were throughout the city, were most effectual in persuading all to listen to the spiritual admonitions of God's holy servant. It was said of him that he had but to look at a sinner, and he could do what he pleased with him. Soon the whole face of the little city was changed. Scandals disappeared. The grace of God triumphed on every side. We will here mention one of the most remarkable of the conversions effected at this time by Saint Gerard.

There was a man dying at Lacedogna whose conscience was loaded with sins. Standing on the threshold of eternity, he had rejected the advances of Priest after Priest who had had the charity to proffer him the consolations of religion.

The whole town was horror-stricken at the spectacle of his obduracy. As everything else had failed, Gerard was at length brought to his bedside. Having first cast one glance at the sick man, he immediately fell on his knees, and, turning to Her whom we all love to salute as the hope of the hopeless, said aloud one "Hail, Mary." He then rose and turned to address the poor sinner. But grace had already done its blessed work. Gerard's look, Gerard's voice, above all, Gerard's prayer, had won the day at last. Satan was driven, routed from the field. The dying man asked earnestly for a Priest, and was happily reconciled with his Eternal Judge.

Whilst he was at Lacedogna, many sick persons were brought to the Saint from Bisaccia, a little town in the immediate neighbourhood, that, if it so pleased God, they might be released from their maladies. But such inhabitants of Bisaccia as were suffering from the prevalent epidemic could not bear the journey to Lacedogna. Gerard, on his side, had the heart of a mother for the sick and miserable. He could not listen to the tale of so much suffering and remain untouched. Accordingly, in deference to repeated entreaties, he went to Bisaccia. Although he could not remain there for any length of time, his stay, short as it was, proved to be full of blessings for the people of the place. Many were the sick persons whom he restored to health. A case which deserves especial mention is that of Bartholomew Melchior. Shortly after his marriage this poor man fell into some species of consumption. One effect of this illness was that he seemed to have almost lost the right use of his reason. He was given over to an evil spirit of gloom and dark despair that settled on him like a cloud of darkness. The unfortunate being had been taken by his friends to a shrine of Saint Antony; but the great Saint Antony in Heaven had remained deaf to their appeals, wishing to reserve this work of mercy for a Saint on earth. As soon as Gerard looked on the poor sufferer, he addressed him cheerfully in a tone of confidence:

"It is nothing, my friend, it is nothing."

He then said a few prayers, his hand gently resting on the head of Bartholomew, who was cured on the spot. Once more he was a man sound both in mind and body.

The epidemic had now abated its violence, and Gerard returned quietly to Iliceto, having accomplished his appointed work after the manner and with the power of a Saint. Virtue had gone out from him, for he walked with God and was perfect.

HIS INTERIOR LIFE

I t is time that we should turn aside from Saint Gerard's deeds of miracle and goodness to the study of his inner life, which was hidden with Christ in God. This was the source of all his activity, the secret of his power over the hearts of men. Fortunately there is no need of drawing upon our imagination in searching even into the depths of his soul. Our Saint shall speak for himself. On the plea of wishing to examine whether he was really guided by the Spirit of God, one of his Directors required him to commit to writing his mortifications, his good desires, his resolutions – all that concerned his spiritual life. Gerard obeyed with the simplicity of a true child of God. The document in which he unconsciously draws the picture of his sanctity with his own hand still remains to us. From it we will now quote:

"Your Reverence is anxious to know in detail the mortifications that I practise, as well as my wishes, feelings, and good resolutions: likewise the exact meaning of the Vow which I have taken always to do that which is most perfect. Behold me, then, ready to give an account, not only of my external actions, but also of all that passes within me, in order to unite myself the more closely with God, and thus walk with greater security in the way of Eternal Salvation."

He then proceeds to give a long list of the mortifications which he practised – some every day, some on Wednesdays, Fridays, and Saturdays; others on special occasions, such as the Novenas preceding great Feasts. From the enumeration of his corporal penances – penances which prove that he was hardly, if at all, surpassed in the matter of personal austerity by any of the Saints – Saint Gerard goes on to his good desires. These he sums up as follows:

To love God, to love Him much.
Always to be united to God.
To do all things for the sake of God.
To be always conformed to His Holy Will.
To suffer much for God.

Having next spoken of his great desires to become a Saint, and after recalling the solemn truth that the abundant opportunities given us during life for the work of our sanctification, being once lost, are lost forever, Gerard goes on thus to apostrophize himself:

"Brother Gerard, make up thy mind to give thyself up to God altogether. From the present moment be thou well convinced, and never forget that to become a Saint one thing alone is necessary – prayer and unbroken contemplation. The best contemplation consists in being as God pleases, in doing the Will of God without reserves, and in spending thyself freely every moment of thy life for the love of God. This, then, is what the Lord demands of thee. Be not a slave of the world or of thyself. It is enough to have God present, to be always united to Him. Most true I hold it that all which is done for God becomes a prayer. Some undertake one thing, some another; my only undertaking must be to do the Will of God. All pain vanishes when we act for God."

We now come to Saint Gerard's great series of resolutions. They deserve to be most carefully meditated. As we study them, we see unrolled before us that love of God and man which was the mainspring of all his energy and strength. Here we may recognize the very kernel of all his sanctity. So practical and so full of spiritual common sense are they, that we may one and all find in some of these resolutions matter, not merely for admiration, but also for everyday imitation in the conduct of our lives.

"My Lord Jesus Christ, behold me in Thy sight, ready to write down, and to promise Thy Divine Majesty that I will faithfully observe these my resolutions. It is long since I first made them. Now with the permission I have received, I confirm them all. Grant, Lord, that I may be found faithful. Woe is me! I cannot trust in myself, unable as I am of myself to perform the smallest undertaking. But I trust solely in Thee, Who art Infinite Goodness and Mercy, and Who canst never but prove faithful to Thy Promises, O Thou supreme Goodness! Whenever I have failed, the - failure came from myself alone. Henceforth I will that Thou shouldst act in me. Grant, I beg of Thee, that I may observe all exactly and without fail – of Thee do I confidently hope to obtain this grace, O Thou inexhaustible Treasure of Mercy.

I choose the Holy Spirit to be my only comforter and protector in all things. May He be my defence, and root out all my faults."

Saint Gerard then entreats the Holy Mother of God and all the citizens of the heavenly country, "especially his patrons, Teresa, Mary Magdalene of Pazzi, and Agnes," to lend him their aid in his endeavour. He proceeds as follows:

"I will examine my conscience every fortnight to see whether I may not have failed in keeping any of the resolutions which I am about to write down. Gerard, know well that one day all that thou now writest will again be brought before thy view. Think well, therefore, of its careful fulfilment. But who art thou, who art thou, I ask, that dost thus threaten me? Thou speakest the truth, but art thou ignorant that never have I relied upon myself, that I do not rely upon myself, and that upon myself I will never rely! Knowing mine utter wretchedness, never should I rest upon myself. Were I so to do, most certainly I should have lost my head. It is in God and in God alone that I trust and I hope. In His Hands I have placed my whole life that He may do with me that which He pleases. Though then I live, I am without life, since God is my life. In Him alone I find my repose, from Him alone do I look for the help that will enable me to keep the promises which I now make.

"Praised be Jesus and Mary.

"Then follow the resolutions. We think that they do not admit of any curtailment, so give them in full as Gerard wrote them:

"I. O my God and my only Love, today and

every day I give myself up to Thy Good Pleasure. In all temptations and trials, I will say always "Thy will be done." All that Thou mayest ordain for me I will embrace with my whole heart, never ceasing to raise my eyes to Heaven, there to adore the Divine Hands which cast towards me the precious pearls of Thy Most Holy Will.

II. Lord Jesus, I wish to carry out all that is commanded me by my Mother the Holy Catholic Church.

III. My Jesus, through love of Thee I will obey my Superiors as Thy Divine Person made visible to my sight. I will live as though I were no longer myself, striving to conform myself to the judgment and will of those who command me, always certain of finding Thee in them.

IV. Amongst all the virtues which are dear to Thee, O my God, that which I love with a love of predilection is holy Purity. My trust is in Thee, O Infinite Holiness, to preserve me from any thought which might sully the brightness of my soul.

V. I will only speak in three cases: when the glory of God is at stake; when the interests of my neighbour may demand it; or when it is necessary for some personal reason.

VI. At recreation I will speak only when I am spoken to, except in one of the three cases mentioned above.

VII. Instead of any words that I might be tempted to speak to the displeasure of God, I will say: "My Jesus, I love Thee with my whole heart."

VIII. I will say nothing either good or bad about myself. I will act as if there were no such person as I in existence.

IX. I will never excuse myself whatever reason

I may have for doing so, unless any sin against God would result from my silence, or any harm to my fellowman.

X. I will oppose all that which opposes Regular Observance in the Community.

XI. I will never answer when I am blamed, unless I am told to do so.

XII. I will attack no one in conversation, nor will I make any reference to the faults of my neighbours, even by way of a joke.

XIII. I will be careful to excuse everyone, considering in my neighbour the Person of Jesus Christ Himself, Whom the Jews accused, notwithstanding His innocence. I will defend others, especially in their absence.

XIV. If anyone should speak ill of another, I will warn him of his fault, even though he be the Father General.

XV. I will do my utmost to manage that others should be spared any occasion of annoyance.

XVI. If I should notice anyone committing a fault, I will be careful not to correct him in the presence of others. I will speak to him on the matter between ourselves, and in a low tone of voice.

XVII. As soon as I see a Father or Brother in any need of assistance, I will leave all to help him, if I can do so consistently with obedience.

XVIII. I will visit the sick, always with the necessary permission, several times every day.

XIX. Never will I mix myself up with anyone else's business. I will never say that anyone has done anything badly.

XX. Whenever I am told to help others in their work, I will obey the responsible person exactly and without remark. I will never allow myself to say that anything is not done as it should be. Still, when I know from experience how things should be carried out, I will give my advice, but never in the tone of a master.

XXI. When I am joined with others in discharging the duties of the house, however trivial they may be (sweeping the corridors, moving furniture, and the like), I will make it my rule never to be anxious to get the best place or the best things. Conveniences I will yield to others, taking for myself what God may leave me. Thus everyone will be pleased, myself among the rest.

XXII. I will never put myself forward to discharge any duty, but will wait until I am told what to do.

XXIII. In the Refectory I will not look about, unless obliged to do so by duty or charity

XXIV. I will take from the board at meals the plate that is nearest to me without looking at the others.

XXV. In all my interior conflicts, I will be careful not to listen to self-love. If anyone blames or accuses me, I will strive to make all bitter feelings pass gently away. Then tranquillity will reign at the bottom of my soul.

XXVI. My supreme resolution is to give myself unreservedly to God. For this reason I will endeavour to have continually before my eyes this motto: "Be thou deaf, blind, and mute."

XXVII. I will not know the meaning of the words "I will" or "I will not." Only one thing do I desire – Thy good pleasure, O my God, and not mine own. In me, O Lord, may Thy Will, not mine, be done.

XXVIII. To do the Will of God it is necessary that I should give up mine own. I wish to possess God only; if, then, I wish for God alone, it must needs be that I should detach myself from all that is not God.

XXIX. I will have it at heart to seek my own interests in nothing.

XXX. During all the time of silence, I will meditate within my soul on the Passion and Death of Jesus Christ, and on the Sorrows of Mary.

XXXI. May all my prayers, Communions, and all my good works be always applied for the salvation of poor sinners in union with the Precious Blood of Jesus Christ.

XXXII. If anyone is wanting in the patience necessary for him to endure the trials that God sends him, and ask me to help him, I will pray for his intention, and for three days offer up all that I do in order to obtain for him a perfect conformity with the Divine Will.

XXXIII. When I receive my Superior's Blessing, I will consider that it is Jesus Christ himself from whom I am receiving it.

XXXIV. As a general rule I will not ask permission for Holy Communion overnight. I will only ask it the moment before I am going into the church. Thus I shall always keep myself in readiness. If permission be refused me, I will make a Spiritual Communion, when the Priest communicates sacramentally.

XXXV. My thanksgiving after Communion shall last until midday, and my preparation for next day shall be made from midday until six o'clock in the evening.

XXXVI. In visiting the Blessed Sacrament, I

will make the following Acts: "O Lord Jesus, I believe that Thou art present in the Blessed Sacrament, and I adore Thee with all my heart."

"I have the intention of adoring Thee by this
visit wherever Thou art present in the Sacred Host,
and I offer Thee Thy Precious Blood for poor sinners. Also I desire to receive Thee spiritually as
many times as there are sanctuaries on earth in
which Thou dost dwell."

XXXVII. I will make these Acts of the Love
of God. "O my God, I have the intention of offering Thee as many acts of love as have been ever
made Thee by the Most Holy Virgin and all the
Saints in Heaven, as well as by all the Faithful on
earth. I would love Thee as much as Jesus Christ
loves Thee, and as He loved His chosen ones. I
would renew these acts with every beating of my
heart. I offer these my desires to my Mother
Mary."

XXXVIII. I will have all possible veneration
for Priests, beholding in them Jesus Christ Himself,
and striving to be penetrated with the greatness of
their dignity."

From his resolutions, Saint Gerard turned to
the explanation of the wonderful Vow that he had
made always to do that which was most perfect.

Explanation of my Vow. I have obliged myself always to do that which is most perfect. By this I
mean that which seems to me to be the most perfect course to take in the sight of God.

It is an obligation which extends to all my actions, even the smallest, compelling me to perform
them always with the greatest self-renunciation and
the utmost perfection. In order to be freed from

perplexity, I will suppose myself ordinarily to have from your Reverence a general permission for this.

Limits of my Vow. Any actions performed in moments of distraction or through inadvertence do not fall under this Vow. Also I shall not be acting against my Vow in asking for some dispensation when out of the house. I make this reservation in order to avoid any scruple which might hamper the freedom of my actions. I always preserve the power to ask from my Confessor for a dispensation from this Vow. On his side he will always be free to liberate me from it, should this seem good to him.

After the statement of this heroic Vow in all deliberate actions to do the most perfect thing, Saint Gerard proceeded to give a list of his daily practices of piety. He even gave his Director a long list of the Saints whom he venerated as his special patrons, such as those most distinguished for their great devotion to the Sacred Humanity of Our Lord, like Saint Mary Magdalene, Saint Bernard, and Saint Philip Neri; those whose hearts were devoured with zeal for souls as Saint Francis Xavier, and Saint Teresa; or great mystics like Saint Francis of Assisi, and Saint Felix Cantalice.

Finally, he concludes this unveiling of his inmost self by the following words of fire:

"O my God!" he cries out, "that I were able to convert as many sinners as there are grains of sand under the sea and on the earth; as there are leaves upon the trees, plants in the fields, stars in the heavens, rays from the sun, or atoms in the air. Would that I could convert to Thee as many souls as there are creatures in this world!"

HIS GREAT TRIAL

"Have the charity to pray much for me. I stand in great need of prayers."

Thus wrote Saint Gerard, in the spring of 1754, to a Priest with whom he was on terms of intimacy. The next day he was to leave Iliceto for Nocera, the residence of Saint Alphonsus. A most cruel accusation had just been made against his good name, and the Holy Founder had summoned him into his own presence to meet it as best he could.

It would seem that Saint Alphonsus never gave full credence to this odious calumny, but as yet he knew but little of Gerard, and the evidence against him appeared to be overwhelmingly strong. When the poor Brother arrived at Nocera, he was at once acquainted with the nature of the charge that had been brought against his character. He listened to all without a word, though, of course, he would have been perfectly free to justify himself had he so pleased.

The rule which forbids a Redemptorist to defend himself when reproved, was never intended to apply to such circumstances as these. But the Servant of God thought of his Vow, always to do that which is most perfect, and determined, in honour of the silence of our Blessed Lord under false accusation, not to say one word in answer to the abominable calumny with which he was assailed. However, his failure to meet or even deny the charge, seemed like a tacit acknowledgment of guilt. Saint Alphonsus was not slow to express his sorrow and indignation. He deprived Gerard of Holy Communion, and forbade him in the strictest manner possible to have any dealings whatsoever with the outside world. The humble Brother bowed his head in meek submission. He accepted all as his due, and never spoke a syllable in self-justification.

On the affair becoming public property, as was soon enough the case, several of the Fathers of the Community, who were well acquainted with Gerard's virtue, begged him to clear himself.

"There is a God in Heaven," was his answer; "He will provide. Would you then deprive me of the opportunity of suffering something for His sake? It is He Who wills that I should endure this humiliation. Ought I not to accomplish His good pleasure? Let God do that which is pleasing to Him. For my part, I desire nothing save that which He desires."

During this season of terrible trial, Saint Gerard redoubled his austerities in order to obtain in more and more abundant measure the help from God, of which he stood in such sore need. His most fervent prayers were those offered for his calumniators. No word of complaint was ever allowed to cross his lips. Not for one moment did he lose his inward serenity of spirit. Forbidden to ap-

proach Holy Communion, which had hitherto
been the one great joy and support of his life, he
used to say gently to those who compassionated
him:

"It is enough for me to have Jesus Christ in my
heart. The Lord wishes to punish the coldness of
my love. He flies away from me, but I possess Him
within my soul by His grace. Never will I lose Him
there."

On being urged to ask permission from Saint
Alphonsus to go once more to Holy Communion,
he hesitated for a moment, but only for a moment.

"No," he said, "I must needs die in the wine-
press of the Will of my God."

Another time he said to a Priest who begged
him to serve his Mass:

"Leave me alone and tempt me not. Did I serve
your Mass, I should snatch Him out of your hands,
as you stand at the Altar."

No other trial that could have been devised
would have been comparable to this trial – the loss
of Holy Communion. It was as though the sun had
suddenly gone down in the heavens, ceasing to
shine upon his earthly life.

Still there were great consolations. God tem-
pers the wind for the shorn lamb. Kind friends who
trusted him throughout with a true-hearted and
loyal trust, which was proof against the most unto-
ward appearances, wrote him letters of affectionate
sympathy and encouragement, that he could not
fail to value highly. But the Holy Spirit, the Comforter, was Himself His servant's supreme Consoler
in this his hour of dire distress.

During the years of his triumphs, when ecstasies and miracles were habitual with him, when

he was held in the universal esteem of his fellow-men, and regarded by all who knew him as a marvellous Saint, he was being purified the while in the crucible of terrible interior sufferings. Men called him the spoiled favourite of Heaven, and he all the time, though they knew it not, was a prey to mysterious trials, known in all their intensity only to the greatest of God's chosen servants.

The fear lest, in punishment of that which his tender conscience deemed his infidelities to grace, he should be cast away from the Presence of the Divine Majesty for all Eternity, haunted him by night and gave him no peace by day. A darkness that could be felt enveloped his soul. Would it truly ever be his to see the Beautiful Face of Jesus Christ? Would it ever be his to stand with Prophets and with Martyrs, with the Forerunner of the Messias, with Virgins and with Confessors, with the Apostles of the Lamb, with the great Foster-Father of Our Lord and the Immaculate Mother of God herself, in the Ranks of the Redeemed round about the Throne of the Eternal? Dared he raise his hopes to such a height as this? And then there came from Satan a dark temptation – the full anguish of which can only be realized by those who love God with the love of the Saints – the temptation to despair. Never for one moment did he yield, though the onslaughts of the enemy seemed to rend his very heart in twain.

"As the gold is tried in the fire, so is the acceptable man in the furnace of tribulations."

But now that he was in deep disgrace, even with Saint Alphonsus his Father, now that many looked upon him askance, as upon a hypocrite who had been found out – now was the time of Divine

Compensations. Light and grace flooded his soul with heavenly joy. God seemed once more to speak face to face with His faithful son. The sensible consolations of his childhood were once more renewed. In a different form, indeed, but none the less truly, were they his again. He seemed almost to enjoy the unveiled vision of his God.

Deprived, as we know through no fault of his own, of the true Bread of Life that God in His wondrous love bestows on the wayfarer, lest journeying painfully through the weary desert of human miseries, he faint beneath the burden and heats of the day – deprived of the Blessed Eucharist, Gerard feasted by faith with the Saints above on the Divine Essence Itself, to which he was united more and more closely each hour that passed, drawn ever upwards even to the heights of sublimest contemplation.

He was asked one day how he could live without Communion. He replied immediately:

"I recreate myself in the Immensity of my God."

Thus did he himself experience the truth of the maxim which we find in one of his letters.

"Only suffer for God, and your very sufferings will bring you Heaven on earth."

So true it is that they alone are happy with a perfect happiness who do the Will of God with a perfect freedom and a perfect service, even as it is done before His Throne on high.

After a time, as Gerard still made no sign, Saint Alphonsus sent him to Ciorani, in order to give him a complete freedom of conscience, in case he might wish to go to Confession to a stranger. We thus perceive that he still rested under grave suspicion, and that in the one quarter where he must have felt suspicion the most keenly. A fortnight was spent by Saint Gerard at Ciorani. He was then again removed to another house, and allowed to go to Holy Communion once a week.

But the clouds were soon to break. The wretched calumniators of his innocence were at length touched with remorse. They wrote to acknowledge that their statements had all been a tissue of lies composed at the instigation of the enemy of mankind.

Saint Alphonsus was overwhelmed with joy. He immediately recalled Gerard to Nocera, and declared that the virtues which he had practised during this time of trial were in themselves enough to prove him to be a great Saint.

The Holy Founder once asked Saint Gerard why he had not said so much as one word to prove his innocence.

"Father," answered Gerard, "does not the Rule forbid us to excuse ourselves?"

Saint Alphonsus was touched to the heart.

"Well, well!" he replied, "may God bless you, my son."

On another occasion he said to Gerard:

"You must have been grievously disturbed in your mind at not being able to receive Holy Communion."

"No! indeed, Father," was the reply – worthy of a Saint – "since Jesus Christ did not wish to come to me, how could I be discontented?"

HIS LETTERS

One of the most remarkable features in Saint Gerard's life is his intimate and continual association with various communities of Religious Women. He reformed at least three Convents by his unaided efforts, and the Acts of his Canonization prove that he was unceasingly occupied with the spiritual interests of Nuns. We find him keeping up the closest relations both with whole communities and with individual sisters, visiting them repeatedly, giving conferences at the grille, writing them long letters – in a word, discharging all the functions of a Director of souls, and, it may be added, of a Director who seemed to have plenty of leisure at his command.

Now this is undoubtedly a very striking fact. That, ordinarily speaking, it is not the vocation of a Lay-brother to undertake the direction of consciences, whether of Nuns or Seculars, is obvious and cannot be gainsaid. All that can be urged in explanation is that, in Saint Gerard's case, his conduct was the result of an extraordinary attraction of Divine grace, proved to be such by his humility and obedience, and countersigned by the approbation both of Bishops, who so warmly invited him to visit convents over which they exercised jurisdiction, and of his own Superiors, who gave him the necessary permission. Greater security no man can ever have on earth than the security which comes from an interior call to some work of zeal – the Voice of God within us – together with the sanction of lawful authority – the Voice of God without us. He who possesses the latter is saved from all possibility of delusion with regard to the former.

Such a security was in the highest degree that of Saint Gerard – one of the most obedient and humble of men.

In order the better to understand his spirit, we will let him speak for himself. He was much devoted to the Carmelite Nuns at Ripacandida, of whom we read so often in the life of Saint Alphonsus. Two of Gerard's most marvellous ecstasies had taken place in the parlour of this Convents-one of them in the presence of the whole community to which he was discoursing at the time on the Love of God. He was venerated by all as a great Saint. We need not, therefore, be surprised to find that, when a new Prioress was elected, she begged Saint Gerard for some directions that would aid her in the discharge of the duties which had just devolved upon her. The Servant of God immediately complied with this request, and sent her a long document, from which we will proceed to make some extracts.

"Since the Prioress holds the place of God Himself, she ought to fulfill her office with the greatest watchfulness, if she wishes to be pleasing to our Divine Master, Who has chosen her to govern in His stead. She needs great prudence, and in all things should direct her course according to the Mind that is in Christ Jesus. Her heart should be embalmed with the sweet perfume of all the virtues which she will communicate to her subjects. They ought to advance to perfection simply by treading in the footsteps of their Mother. The Superior will never lose sight of her own lowliness and insufficiency, remembering that God has raised her to the position which she occupies, of His mere Goodness, since there are so many others who would acquit themselves more perfectly than she. Thus, abasing herself in her own eyes, she will have compassion on the faults of others. She will discharge the duties of her office in the spirit of love, and will never look upon it as too painful to be endured. Considering that God from all Eternity has destined her to be in authority, let her day by day strive to be a better Superior, keeping herself always united to the Divine Will, and holding her position with a total indifference, and without the slightest attachment.

"In cases of difficulty she ought no doubt to get the best advice within reach. But having once made up her mind, she must propose to herself the Glory of God as the end to be attained, and carry out her resolves without any human respect, even though she had to shed the last drop of her blood. For the love of God she must trample self-love under foot.

The Superior ought often to say to herself: 'God wishes me where I am. I ought then to do His Holy Will in all things. As a duty I will Watch over all my daughters; I will be the servant of all. I must give each one advice, light, consolation. To others I should assign that which is best, keeping for myself that which is worst, in order that I may please God. In a word, everywhere and in all things I must suffer in order to be a faithful disciple of Jesus Christ, my heavenly Spouse.'

"The mind of a Superior should be like a wheel, always in motion, that she may provide for the needs of her daughters. She will love them all dearly, but only in God, without showing any preference to one rather than to another. Remembering that Nuns can provide nothing for themselves excepting in accordance with Holy Obedience, she ought to forget herself completely, and devote all the gifts that God has given her to their service. If any presents should be sent into the Convent from outside, let her provide for the wants of all her children before she thinks of her own.

"She ought to put them all at their ease, particularly any who may be in danger of failing in confidence towards her. To do this she must win their hearts. She will therefore be affable in her manner, even when she feels it to be most difficult, and must continually strive to overcome herself in this respect – always with a view to please God. Unless she acts after this fashion, unless she shows a mother's love to those who are suffering from temptation, their disturbance of mind will go on increasing. It may even throw them into despair. At least they will be prevented from advancing in the Love of God by the feeling that they are being slighted or misunderstood. This is a weakness to which women are subject."

The Saint then continues to speak of the firmness and sweetness, but especially the sweetness, with which corrections should be made, and concludes thus:

"Such a correction is, in my opinion, well calculated to induce an imperfect Religious to have recourse with much confidence to her Superior, who may thus be able to rescue her from her tepidity, and restore her to the path of perfection. We also gain more by sweetness than by harshness. Harshness brings trouble, temptation, obscurity, and spiritual sloth in its train. Sweetness, on the contrary, gives peace and tranquillity. It disposes the soul for union with God. If all Superiors were to follow these Rules, all subjects would become Saints. It is the want of prudence that causes so much trouble in certain Religious Houses. Where disturbance reigns, there reigns the Evil One; and where Satan reigns, there God is not to be found."

It was to these Carmelite Nuns, whose Prioress received this striking admonition, that Gerard had written some few years previously:

"How earnestly do I desire that all the dear Sisters should dwell for ever in the Wounded Heart of Jesus, and in the afflicted Heart of the Blessed Virgin. It is in these Hearts that there is to be found all sweetness. In these Hearts may we find our Rest."

On one occasion he wrote thus to the Mother Prioress:

"Believe me, my very dear Mother in Jesus Christ, that notwithstanding my unworthiness, I pray continually to the Lord for you and for your community. The whole object of my prayers is to obtain that you may be perfect spouses of the Divine Master and true lovers of His Most Holy Will. I say it in all truth, I never find myself in the Pres-

ence of our Lord without seeing you in His Most
Sacred Heart, and then I offer to God for you and
all your daughters that Sacred Heart, all covered
with Wounds for our sake."

Let us now see how Saint Gerard wrote to a
Novice who, as he heard, was tempted against her
vocation:

"My dear Sister in Jesus Christ, I tell you in the
Name of God that you ought to keep yourself in a
firm and holy peace, for all this tempest is the work
of the Evil One, who is striving to induce you to
leave your holy home. My child, be on your guard.
Satan is full of cunning and envious hatred. He
would prevent you from becoming a Saint. For this
reason your perseverance causes him the greatest
anger. We all of us have experienced his assaults
against our Vocation, but God only permits them
in order to test our faithfulness. Take comfort then.
Offer yourself always to Jesus without reserve, and
He will not fail to come to your assistance. How is
it possible that your love should forget how many
times you have promised Jesus Christ to be His
spouse for ever? If, then, you have so ardently desired this title of spouse of the Divine Master, why
renounce it now? . . . Go on your way therefore in
all freedom of soul. Be bright. Love God with all
your heart. Offer yourself often to Him, and rout
the powers of Hell. One last word. Pray for me. I
do not forget to pray for you."

This letter produced its effect. The Novice was
for ever delivered from her temptations, and became an excellent Religious.

From these short extracts we may form some
conception of the general tone of Saint Gerard's
letters to Nuns, a great number of which have been

preserved to us. They all breathe charity, sweetness, loving-kindness, and are all pervaded with a heavenly unction. His was the gentle spirit of Jesus Christ our Lord.

It was not only to Religious Women that Gerard wrote letters of consolation and advice. Many Priests sought his aid, and he ever regarded it as his greatest privilege to be able to help those whom God had anointed to be the helpers of His people.

Saint Gerard wrote the following to a Priest who consulted him in his perplexities:

"With regard to your scruples about your past life, since you have already made, as I am well aware, on several occasions, a serious examination of conscience, be at rest and trouble yourself no more on this subject. Your doubts arise simply from the wiles of Satan. The Devil is striving, by means of the storm that he has raised within your soul, to make you lose peace of conscience. Be careful, then, not to give ear to his suggestions, regard this inquietude as a real temptation, and keep yourself calm that you may be able to go forward in the way of Perfection.

As for the scruples which have reference to the Confessional, I assure you, with all sincerity, that this is likewise a temptation. The Enemy wishes to make you abandon this occupation, which concerns so nearly the glory of God, and for which you have been chosen from all eternity to the great good of your own soul. In the Name of God, do not give way to any such temptation. If your Reverence were to cease hearing Confessions, your spiritual life would suffer the greatest loss, and in eternity God would not bestow upon you the magnificent reward which He is preparing for you if you are faithful. To abandon the Confessional would be the same thing for you as not to do the Will of God, for the Will of God (I say it again) for you is that you should labour with the greatest zeal in His Vineyard. Do not permit yourself to be further troubled concerning any mistakes which you may commit through inadvertence in the exercise of your Ministry. It is enough that your will should be unswervingly bent on not offending God. For all else, commit yourself to the good keeping of Divine Providence."

Here is a letter written by Saint Gerard to a Redemptorist Father who had asked his advice in his interior trials:

"I am rejoiced and indeed consoled, Reverend Father, at the dealings of Almighty God with your Reverence. I am quite confident that He will grant you the grace to triumph over all your spiritual enemies. Courage, then! Fear nothing, but rather rejoice. The Lord is certainly on your side, and He will never abandon you. Your Reverence has doubts concerning your past Confessions. This is a little trial which God sends you, to give you an opportunity of suffering something for His sake. You tell me that you are yourself responsible for all. You could not think otherwise without your anxiety immediately disappearing. It is thus that the Divine Majesty acts towards the souls whom He loves, permitting them to be persuaded that all comes from their own remissness. If your Reverence once felt that all your sufferings came from the Hand of God, where would be the suffering? You would then find in those very sufferings a Paradise of delights. After all, even if we have some little faults,

and even though we do fall sometimes, let us re-
member that the Saints themselves were flesh and
blood. Trust in God, my dear Father, and hope in
Him. In your charity, recommend me to Jesus
Christ, and His Most Holy Mother Mary. I beg of
Them to bless us both."

HIS WONDERFUL LIFE AT NAPLES

The Redemptorist Fathers were, from an early period in the history of their Congregation, in possession of a small residence in Naples; it had been bestowed upon them by the brother of Saint Alphonsus, so that they might have a home of their own, where they could break the journey when passing through the city from one Mission to another.

Father Margotta, the Procurator General of the Congregation, shortly after the triumphant vindication of Saint Gerard's character, was sent to take charge of this little house. He was a man of exceptional holiness. Well acquainted with the Saint, he had written to him most kindly in his late trouble, and now be begged, as a special favour, that he might be given him as his companion during his stay in Naples.

"Yes," said Saint Alphonsus, "take him with you. It will be some compensation to him after the trials which he has borne so generously."

Father Margotta and Saint Gerard for some months lived together at Naples a life of wonderful sanctity. They were alone, and thus enjoyed the greater liberty to give full vent to their fervour in the heroic service of God. Understanding one another thoroughly, they used to exercise their ingenuity in discovering fresh means whereby they might spur each other on in the practice of virtue. Father Margotta once asked Gerard what he had got ready for their dinner.

"The dinner which your Reverence ordered this morning," was the smiling answer; "that and nothing more!"

There was, it appeared, no dinner whatsoever prepared that day, for none had been ordered! The Saint knew, doubtless, that Father Margotta would be rejoiced to share his fast.

However, it was not always with Father Margotta that he had to deal. A Lay-brother, Francis Tartaglione by name, was sent by his Superiors to pay them a visit at Naples. The morning after his arrival, he and Saint Gerard both went out. It was Gerard's duty to cater for the midday meal. Before he had as yet bought anything, he came upon a wretched huckster selling matches in the market-place. Sad, indeed, was the story of want and misery that he poured into the sympathetic ears that were now open to his tale of woe. He was – so he declared – absolutely dying of hunger. For Gerard to empty his slender purse into the poor man's hands was the work of a moment. He accepted some of his wares in exchange for the money, and then bent his steps homewards in all peace of mind. Meanwhile, Brother Francis had also returned to the house, and when Gerard appeared, he asked him at once what he had got for dinner.

The Servant of God replied with a sly glance:

"God is all that we need: we want nothing more."

"That is all very well," retorted Brother Francis impatiently, " but how about the dinner?"

Before him, on the table, lay the store of matches.

"What may those things be?" he continued in amazement.

"My dear Brother," answered Gerard. "I am sure that we shall find them very useful."

He then told the story of his adventure in the market-place. Poor Brother Francis' discomfiture was complete. He was entirely disarmed, and had not a word to say. Charity, we all know, is the Queen of Virtues; still, try as he might, he could not help feeling that he needed his dinner badly enough.

Soon Father Margotta joined them. Saint Gerard told him at once all that had occurred, saying simply that in the absence of his Superior, he had assumed his permission to give the poor man an alms.

"But," said Father Margotta, noticing, with some amusement, the disconsolate appearance of Brother Francis, "tell us, please, what we are to have to eat today?"

"God will provide," was the only reply that he received. A few moments after there was heard a ring at the bell.

"Perhaps that is our dinner," remarked Father Margotta with a smile.

Brother Gerard and he went together to the door. Father Margotta had prophesied! There, before their eyes, stood a servant with a basketful of eatables! She had just been told by her mistress to take a present to the Redemptorists, though she merely knew them by name. We may be sure that Brother Francis never forgot how God thus set the seal of His Divine Approval upon Saint Gerard's charity.

During the first few weeks of his stay at Naples, the holy Brother gave himself up without let or hindrance to the practice of prayer and contemplation. His duties in the house being very slight, the greater part of the day was at his own disposal.

Father Margotta said Mass every day in the Church of the Oratorian Fathers. After Mass, Gerard used to spend the whole morning, hidden away in a corner, generally stretched as though lifeless on the pavement. He also visited with great assiduity any church in which the Blessed Sacrament was exposed for the Forty Hours' Adoration.

But throughout Saint Gerard's life we see how irresistible was his attraction for works of chanty. This soon manifested itself at Naples. No great length of time had elapsed before he was well known in the city. Every day he was to be found in the public hospitals ministering to the sick, after the example set him by his holy Father Saint Alphonsus; in the lunatic asylums consoling the poor inmates with his sweet kindness; in the big shops winning the hearts of the young men there employed to the love of Our Lord Jesus Christ. Great were the conversions that he thus effected, and numerous were the sinners whom he led to the feet of Father Margotta, that they might be absolved from their sins in the Sacrament of Penance.

As usual, his sanctity was illustrated by the gift of miracles. One of the most wonderful that he ever performed belongs to this period of his life. It has been attested on oath by a large number of eyewitnesses. Standing one day by the Bay of Naples, he noticed a great crowd of men. and women. They were rending the air with their piercing shouts of terror. A storm had suddenly arisen with great violence. A boat was on the point of sinking beneath the waves. Full of compassion for these poor people, and relying upon the protecting Arm of Him Who quelled the storm of old, and caused Saint Peter to walk upon the face of the waters as upon solid earth, Gerard made the sign of the Cross, and then advanced unhesitatingly into the sea.

"In the Name of the Most Holy Trinity," thus did he adjure the frail craft which was going down before his very eyes, "stay where thou art, I command thee."

That moment the boat remained motionless. Gerard advanced, seized it, as he might have caught a lily floating upon the surface of the Bay, and brought it to the shore. Then, in presence of the assembled multitude, without his clothes being so much as wet, he stepped out of the sea on to dry land.

The people in enthusiastic wonderment cried out:

"A miracle! A miracle!"

Gerard himself in his humility ran away, as though he had committed some great crime, and hid himself in a shop until nightfall. When Father Margotta asked him afterwards how he had managed to draw in the boat, he answered simply:

"Father, to God all things are possible."

The renown of this miracle caused Gerard to

become known in every part of Naples. He could
not appear in the streets without men and women
calling out as he passed:

"There goes the Saint! The Saint who saved
the boat."

The little Redemptorist House was daily besieged by persons of all ranks, eager to speak to the
holy Brother, and obtain his advice in their troubles
and difficulties. But the more he was exalted
among men, the more earnestly did Gerard set
himself to discover fresh means of self-abjection.

When he first went to Naples he used, sometimes alone, sometimes with Father Margotta –
who seems to have been almost as greedy of humil-
iations as himself – to mix with the beggars at the
door of the Oratory. Then with the other poor
people he would ask an alms of the chanty of the
sons of Saint Philip. This wonderful act of humility was of course forbidden directly it came to
the ears of higher Superiors at a distance, but
Gerard soon found other means of advancing in
holy humility.

Thus, one day, on opening the door, he received the following message:

"The Duchess of Maddoloni wishes to see
Brother Gerard."

As he saw that the servant evidently did not
know him by sight, he replied in all seriousness:

"I am afraid that I cannot bring you that
Brother. To tell you the truth, he is only a simpleton and a fool. People, as I find, are strangely
mistaken about him here at Naples. Please tell the
Duchess so from me."

This lady had wished to see Saint Gerard that
she might obtain at his hands the cure of a sick

child. When the servant brought back the answer that he had received, she knew at once that it could have come from no other than the Saint himself.

Early the next morning she went to the Church of the Holy Spirit, where she knew that she would be sure to find Saint Gerard. As soon as she saw him come in, she went up to him and begged of him to obtain from God the recovery of her child.

"There," said Gerard, turning his eyes to the tabernacle, "there dwells the Giver of all good gifts."

"It is from you and from Him," replied the Duchess, "that this grace on which I have set my heart must come."

Gerard bowed to her, and promised to pray for her child. The poor mother was still in the church when her maid came in quickly to tell her that the little girl had been suddenly cured. It was subsequently ascertained that the cure took place at the very moment when our Saint had promised to recommend the child to God.

Ladies living in the world were far from being the only persons to seek the help of Saint Gerard. In Naples, as elsewhere, Priests and Religious vied with one another in the eagerness with which they strove to obtain his advice, until at last his Superiors felt bound to interpose.

It might be dangerous, even for Gerard – a Lay-brother by vocation – thus to be made the idol of a great city. Again, it was hardly conducive to the calm, which should pervade a Religious House, that the little Redemptorist Residence should become a centre of attraction for crowds of eager visitors, anxious even at the most inconvenient hours to see the marvellous worker of miracles, with whose fame all Naples was ringing. Accordingly, after a stay of about four months' duration in the capital, Gerard was, to his own great contentment, attached by Saint Alphonsus to the House of Caposele, and thus restored once more to the ordinary Community life of a Redemptorist Lay-brother.

HE IS CALLED FATHER OF
THE POOR

S aint Gerard, on reaching his destination, was
given the office of porter. Remembering that
fidelity to the duties of one's state is the surest
means of sanctification, the holy Brother said smil-
ingly, but in all earnestness, that the key which now
opened the hall door must also one day open wide
for him the gates of Paradise.

Perhaps, next to the office of sacristan, none
could have been more congenial to Gerard than
that of porter, for in this capacity it was his lot to
provide for the necessities of the poor, who sought
relief at the convent door. Throughout life he had
been noted for his charity to those in need. With
vivid faith he saw in them the Person of Our Lord
Himself, and was accustomed to say that the poor
were the Visible Christ, even as the Blessed Sacrament was the Christ Invisible.

"Our house at this time," writes Father Tannoia, "was besieged with beggars. The holy porter
had the same anxiety for their good that a mother
has for the well-being of her children. He pos-
sessed the art of always sending them away satis-

fied, and neither their unreasonableness nor their deceitful tricks ever made him lose patience."

He was doubly anxious to assist such of them as were sick. If they were too ill to come themselves, and sent their children for food, he did all in his power to supply their wants to the full. He knew them all, and, when he went out, used to visit them in their own homes.

Those who had seen better days, who were now in need, but were ashamed to ask openly for relief, were before all others the objects of his solicitude. We are told that he supported whole families of this class. Funds never seemed to be wanting to him for any good work. He hoped in God and was not disappointed.

There was a general failure of crops in the year 1754, with the result that there was great want throughout the country. By the end of December two hundred poor persons, men, women and children, came daily for alms to the convent door. Their state was rendered all the more pitiable from an exceptionally hard winter, which added to this distress that was already sufficiently great. Under the circumstances the Father Rector gave the porter full powers.

"I charge you," he said, "to provide for the wants of these poor people. Their fate is in our hands. If we do not help them, I do not know what is to become of them. Take anything that is in the house, and do with it as you think best."

Thus given a free hand, Gerard threw himself with the utmost devotedness into the work. It was a cold winter and they were wellnigh naked. Relying on the general permission that he had received, he went to the Community wardrobe, laid hands on everything he could find, and had clothes made for his poor clients. During all that inclement season, he kept nothing for himself but an old worn habit. His cloak and everything he could possibly spare he had long ago given away.

INDEED THE COLD that year was excessive, so that oftentimes he would light a fire in the hall in order to warm the shivering creatures who would gather round it, blessing God and Brother Gerard. The sight of the little children whom their parents sometimes brought to the convent, all benumbed with cold, touched him to the quick. Tears of compassion coursed down his cheeks as he took their poor little hands and chafed them in his own, remembering the love of Jesus for innocent children.

But it was not enough to clothe the naked; it was necessary also to feed the hungry. This would have been impossible had not Divine Providence again and again come to Saint Gerard's aid. He who fed five thousand men with five small loaves showed once more that His arm was not shortened. Everyone, both in the Community and outside of it, knew that bread multiplied miraculously in Gerard's hands.

Thus, a young Redemptorist cleric related that once he was watching the distribution of food by the marvellous Brother, when, to his utter amazement, he observed that directly the baskets were emptied they were immediately refilled, without any human being placing in them anything more whatsoever.

Oftentimes this miraculous multiplication of

food was witnessed by a large number of other persons, as well as by those of his own household.

He had, with the help of the other Brothers, prepared a little feast for his poor people, a sumptuous dish of macaroni, loved by every true Italian. They thought that enough had been prepared and to spare, but there were more guests than Gerard had anticipated. It became clear that the supply would run short. Everyone felt uncomfortable excepting the Saint. He went on quietly giving everyone an ample helping, and wonderful to relate, when all were satisfied, there was still macaroni left upon the dish. It had been multiplied before their very eyes.

One day Saint Gerard gave away every morsel of bread in the house, so that not so much as a single loaf remained for the Community supper. When the Brother who had charge of the baking discovered this, he was, as may easily be imagined, in a great state of concern, and went off to the Father Rector to complain. The Rector sent for Gerard, and blamed him in the presence of the other Brother for what he had done, especially as it was now too late in the day to buy bread in the town.

"Fear not, Father," replied Gerard, "God will provide."

Then turning to the Brother, he added: "Brother, let us go and see; perhaps there is still some left."

"No," the other said impatiently, "there most certainly is not. If you like, I will let you see for yourself."

Gerard followed him to the bread-chest.

"Now," said the Brother, before raising the lid,

"now you will find that there is not a crumb to be seen."

With these words he opened the chest. Behold it was quite full!

"God be ever blessed," cried out Gerard, and immediately ran away to the church, there to thank the goodness of his Lord.

"Oh!" gasped the other Brother to the Father Rector, who had just appeared on the scene, "Gerard is a real Saint. To think that I should have ventured to complain of him! When I left this place to go to you, I assure your Reverence that there was not one loaf left, not one, and now the chest is full. God must have done this."

"Yes, it is God Who has done it," answered the Rector. "Let us, then, leave Gerard alone, for of a truth Our Lord is pleased to play with him."

Sometimes Almighty God deigned even to create bread for His servant that so he might relieve the poor. There are two recorded instances of this.

Laurence Miniello, an artisan of the neighbourhood, could not find food for his two young daughters during the general distress. Accordingly he sent them to Gerard, whose charity he knew to be unfailing. One day they happened to arrive rather later than usual. The Servant of God had finished his distribution, and had nothing left to give them. He was greatly grieved at their disappointment. Then pausing to think, he turned away, went inside the Convent for an instant, and came back with two little loaves of bread in his hands, still piping hot. The children could hardly believe their eyes. He had been only away a minute. They knew that no one could have given him these loaves, which were indeed of a different size and shape from those baked in the Convent. They fully believed them to be miraculous, and told their father, all about it on their return home.

This same marvel was repeated on behalf of a respectable woman, who, pressed by the pangs of hunger, took her place one day at the door. Overcome by shame, she did not like to ask for relief, and held back bashfully from the crowd. After having finished the usual distribution of food, Gerard went away, pretending not to see this person. He thought that she had not come out of any necessity, but from curiosity, as did many of the inhabitants, to watch the wonders which so often took place. On being told the real state of the case, the Saint was deeply moved.

"Why, why," he said, "was I not told before?" Then he reflected a minute, went back into the house, and immediately returned to take out of the folds of his habit a little loaf, quite hot, as if it had just come out of the oven. As in the case of the loaves given to the children, it was of a much finer quality than the bread in the convent. Besides, it was found that the oven was cold, and that the fire had not been lighted all the day.

Thus was Gerard wondrously enabled during that hard winter to provide for the wants of the starving people of Caposele. He was in truth the Father of the Poor.

WITH FATHER MARGOTTA
AGAIN

With the spring the bitterly cold weather passed away at Caposele, and plenty once more smiled upon the land. Meanwhile Father Margotta at Naples was always asking to have the holy Brother with him again, and, as it might be hoped that the excitement caused by Gerard's miracles had by this time somewhat subsided, Saint Alphonsus did not hesitate to accede to his request. Father Margotta, who was visiting the Convent of Caposele, took Brother Gerard away with him. On their way to Naples business took them to Calitri, Father Margotta's native place. As our Saint was unknown here, for some few days he was left in peace, and allowed to satisfy his thirst for prayer before the Blessed Sacrament. But it was not long before a woman arrived at the house of the Parish Priest, with whom the two Redemptorists were staying, and asked for Brother Gerard. She was from Bisaccia, the little place where, as it will be remembered, the Servant of God had displayed so much charity and worked so many miracles during an epidemic. Her object in her present visit was to obtain the cure of a relation who was seriously ill.

On being told that Gerard was out, she said that she would await his return. When he came in, she threw herself at his feet, and in a voice broken with sobs, begged of his charity the favour on which her heart was set. Saint Gerard listened to her with his usual kindness, consoled her in her trouble, and assured her that it would be done unto her even as she wished.

Naturally enough the people of the house could not understand this scene at all, and on the appearance of Father Margotta, the whole story was related with much merriment for his special delectation. Their surprise may be imagined when they were told that their amusement proceeded from their ignorance of the gifts which God had bestowed upon his companion. In order to clear Gerard from conclusions injurious to his good sense and humility, which otherwise must have been drawn from his late conduct, Father Margotta proceeded to recount the tale of his virtues and miracles.

It was enough. Soon Calitri was all agog with excitement about the marvellous wonder-worker whom Divine Providence had sent amongst them.

An excellent medical man of the locality, Giovanne Cioglia by name, was very ill. He had received the last Sacraments, and been given up by the doctors. Saint Gerard was invited to go and see him. At first he refused. In this refusal he persisted, until Father Margotta brought his authority to bear in the matter. The Saint then went as he was told. Finding the patient unconscious, he made the sign of the Cross upon his forehead, when immediately the sick man recovered the use of his senses, and found himself restored to perfect health. The bystanders cried out: "A miracle!" but Gerard answered simply:

"Behold what obedience can do!"

A lady of Calitri discovered the sanctity of the Servant of God in a singular manner. One day she had a violent headache. Happening to be in the Priest's house, she saw Saint Gerard's hat in a corner of the room.

"Let me see," she said, half in earnest, half in jest, "whether this Brother is the Saint that people say."

She then put the hat on her own head. Immediately she was freed from her headache.

This fact being noised abroad, some persons managed to induce Gerard to accept a present of new shoes. They kept the old ones as a relic. These shoes of Brother Gerard were for many a year lent from house to house in Calitri, and numerous were the cures that God granted to sick persons who used them with faith, imploring the powerful intercession of His servant Gerard.

When Father Margotta's business was accomplished at Calitri, he went straight to Naples. On returning once more to the spot that had been the theatre of so many of his marvels, Saint Gerard was more careful than ever to keep himself as far as possible in the background, and avoid anything that might bring him again, without absolute necessity, into prominence. One day he was speaking with a friend outside the church of the Holy Spirit, when two ladies came up to him.

"My dear Brother Gerard," said one of them, with tears in her eyes, "come, I beg of you, and cure my poor child."

At first he refused, but unable to resist a mother's prayer, he said:

"Very well, but I must first go and get permission."

When on his visit the child was cured, it was to Obedience that he gave the glory.

If in Saint Gerard's gentle character there was any trace of severity that was not reserved for himself, it was directed towards imposture or pretence, which his soul detested. Near the Redemptorist residence a beggar took his stand each day to ask for alms. To all appearance his was a sad case. He hobbled along on crutches, and one of his legs was wrapped round and round with bandages. Gerard, however, knew that he was a good-for-nothing wretch, who, through laziness, was imposing on the charity of the people. So he told him several times to move away. But as all was useless, at last the Saint tore the bandages off his limbs by main force, and said with great severity:

"You are a swindler and a cheat. If you wish to save your soul, cease mocking God and deceiving men."

The cripple was a cripple no longer. He ran away as fast as he could go, using both his legs, and leaving his crutches behind him.

After some six weeks spent at Naples, Father Margotta was ordered by his Superiors to make a new foundation in the diocese of Benevento. Thus he and Saint Gerard were again to be separated. Gerard returned for a short time to Calitri, where a Mission was at the time being preached – then back again to Caposele. At Calitri he worked innumerable conversions. If the Fathers were kept busy during the whole Mission in hearing the confessions of the people, he was occupied in preparing sinners for the worthy reception of the Holy Sacraments. This work we know was one especially dear to his loving heart. The zeal for the House of the Lord had eaten him up – zeal for that spiritual Temple which is formed by the Holy Ghost in the souls of men.

NEW MARVELS

S aint Gerard was only thirty years of age, yet he was already completely worn out. His whole life had been devoted to prayer – oftentimes continued for long hours far into the night – to the severest bodily austerities, and to hard physical labour. Still, exhausted though he felt, he never relaxed his efforts: never for one instant did he dream of repose – his great ambition was to work on uncomplainingly even to the end, until the night should come when he could work no longer. Did charity or duty call on him to sacrifice himself, he was always found eager to answer to the call.

As though to reward the generosity of His servant, Almighty God now loaded him with gifts and graces in an ever-increasing abundance. It was especially towards the close of his life that Gerard manifested his power of "Bilocation," that is to say of being seen in two places at the same time.

At Lacedogna there lived a family called Di Gregorio, with whom the Saint was on terms of special intimacy. He had one day worked a striking miracle on their behalf, restoring to its unimpaired condition a large cask of wine, which had turned acid.

Now it so happened that a servant in this house became dangerously ill. One evening in the midst of her pain she remembered this miracle, thought of Saint Gerard, and ardently desired to see him.

"Oh, my dear Brother Gerard!" she cried out, "where are you? Why do you not come and deliver me from my sufferings?"

The words were hardly out of her mouth before she heard a knock at the door. It was Gerard himself. He went straight up to her and said: "You called me; I am here to be of service to you. Have you a lively faith in God? If so, be cured!"

He then made the sign of the Cross upon the girl's forehead, and left her without another word. Her pains had vanished; she got up quite well. Needless to say, her first anxiety was to thank her wonderful benefactor. But he was nowhere to be found. On inquiry it transpired that he had been seen by no one in the place outside of the Di Gregorio household. Except for that supernatural visit to the sick-room he had not been at Lacedogna all the day.

On another occasion Saint Gerard had a long conversation with a great friend of his, a very charitable man, called Theodore Clem. Before leaving the Saint, Theodore promised to prepare a list of the most necessitous persons in Caposele and bring it to the convent. On his way home he went into a cottage, where he knew that there was a man who was very ill and in a state of extreme destitution. On being asked by his visitor of what he stood in the greatest need, the poor sufferer replied cheerfully:

"I need nothing, for Brother Gerard has been with me a short time ago. He has relieved all my wants."

Theodore's surprise may be imagined. For the moment he was dumbfounded; then he said bluntly that that was certainly untrue, as he had himself been with Brother Gerard in the convent, at the very time that he was supposed to be paying this visit of charity. But when the sick man persisted in his assertion, and in confirmation thereof produced the presents that the holy Brother had just made him, there was no longer any room for reasonable doubt, at least in the mind of one who knew the gifts and sanctity of the Servant of God. It was clearly a case of Bilocation.

Father Tannoia, than whom no one had better opportunities of knowing the truth, and whose evidence is beyond suspicion, tells us that Saint Gerard made frequent use of this most marvellous endowment. Thus once, on not receiving some news that he expected from Muro, he said quietly:

"I must go there tomorrow."

It was afterwards stated on unexceptionable authority that he was seen in Muro the next day, although, on the other hand, it is equally certain that he did not leave the convent at Caposele.

The mysterious presence of the Saint in more than one place at the same moment of time was sometimes both effected and apprehended, not visibly, but in a spiritual manner. He was, as we know, throughout his life often supernaturally apprised of events occurring at a distance, and towards the end, as he became more and more emancipated from the shackles of the flesh, the sphere of his soul's activity was so enlarged by

Almighty God that he was able to make his advent felt among his friends who were – as regards the body – far away from him at the time. We may easily believe that the impression made upon the minds of those whom he thus visited was more vivid and more lasting than would have been the case had his presence been recognized merely according to the manner with which custom has rendered us all familiar.

Thus Dr. Santorelli, the medical attendant of the Community, and a great friend of Saint Gerard, made the following statement:

"As I was one day making my usual round of visits to my patients, wherever I went I felt Brother Gerard by my side as really as if I had seen him with my eyes. My duties finished, I went to the convent, and on meeting him, I asked him: 'What were you about accompanying me in that fashion all the morning?'"

"'Do you not know,' he answered, 'that I have to go away tomorrow? so I wished to visit all my poor people with you before leaving.'"

Santorelli's own family once experienced a somewhat similar marvel. Saint Gerard was at their house, and on leaving he said that he would come back in the evening. The doctor smiled, as he knew that it was against the rules of the house for him to go out without necessity after the evening Angelus.

"I am not joking," said the Brother; "I will come back, not in the body but in the spirit."

As a matter of fact, that night Dr. Santorelli's sister, Monica, saw Gerard fixing his searching gaze upon her. She said that she was ready to declare, upon oath if necessary, that it was no mere imagination, but that she had really seen the holy Brother.

The lives of the Saints show us that some of God's chosen servants have received from Him the gift of rendering themselves invisible to the eyes of men.

This extraordinary favour was not refused to Saint Gerard. He was once making his monthly Retreat, when the Father Rector, chancing to require his services, sent for him to his room. Gerard was not there. They looked in the oratory. He was not there either. The whole house was searched from top to bottom. All was in vain. He was nowhere to be found. Meanwhile Dr. Santorelli called. The Rector hastened to tell him the news. Brother Gerard was lost.

Santorelli laughingly suggested:

"Perhaps he has hidden under the bed to be quiet on his Retreat day. Let us go and look."

Taking a Brother with him, the Doctor went himself to Gerard's room, but all to no purpose.

"It does not matter," said Santorelli on his return. He knew Saint Gerard well, and added: "When the time for Communion comes, you will see that he will leave his hiding-place."

So it happened. Gerard duly appeared in the church to receive Holy Communion. After his thanksgiving, the Father Rector asked him where he had been all the morning.

"In my room," was the answer.

"In your room!" rejoined the Rector. "We went there twice to look for you!"

Gerard said nothing, but only smiled.

However, on being told to explain this seeming contradiction, he said with all simplicity:

"As I feared to be disturbed in my Retreat, I begged of Our Lord the grace to become invisible."

"This once I forgive you," said his Rector, "but see that you do not make such prayers in future."

Saint Gerard's room had no furniture excepting a small table and a bed. There was nothing that could have (naturally speaking) prevented him from being seen. We can only exclaim that God is wonderful in His Saints, and that He will refuse nothing to their prayers.

It sometimes happened that Gerard exercised his supernatural gifts in circumstances that will appear almost trivial if we fail to remember that, when there is question of doing a kind act, nothing is trivial in the sight of God.

Thus one day meeting a lady named Candida Fongarelli, he asked her to give him a little white silk out of which to make a veil for a ciborium. She said that of course she would be delighted, and on her return home did her best to find what was wanted. However, not succeeding, she made up her mind to cut it out of her wedding-dress. Next day Gerard saw her again, and told her at once, before she alluded to the subject at all, that she was not to spoil her wedding-dress for the sake of two little pieces of silk. He said that if she made a fresh search he was sure that she would find what would serve his purpose. The lady was thunderstruck at seeing him thus disclose a secret intention which she had not made known to any human being. On her return home, acting on Gerard's advice, she looked again, found the silk, as he had told her would be the case, and brought it to him at the convent.

One day after Holy Communion the Saint withdrew to make his thanksgiving before a large crucifix. He was at this time discharging the office of cook in the Community. But rapt in contemplation on the Passion of Our Lord, he allowed the hours to glide by, until the bell rang for dinner without his having left the Oratory where he was praying. They looked for him all over the house. When at last he was found, the Brother said to him:

"Gerard, what have you been about? The bell has rung for dinner, and the kitchen is locked."

"Man of little faith," replied Gerard, "what had the Angels to do all the while?"

To the amazement of the whole house, the dinner that day was like one given on great Feast days. Our Lord had called His servant to spend the morning in loving colloquy with Himself. It was impossible that others should suffer from his obedience to the Voice of God. His conduct, due to an extraordinary inspiration, was thus, even by miracle, stamped with the Divine approval.

Greater and greater waxed the Saint's power over the hearts of men, as the end drew near. One notable conversion in particular belongs to this period of his life. The Archbishop of Conza had come to spend a few days with the Redemptorist Fathers, and had brought with him his confidential secretary, a Roman by birth – a man full of wit and merriment. But this exterior light -heartedness was only the cloak of interior misery. His conscience was in a deplorable state. Gerard had hardly seen him when by a Divine light he knew all. At once he determined to win this soul for God. Accordingly, he deliberately put himself in the way of the secretary. Whenever he met him, he used to chat with him, laughing at his jokes and encouraging his witticisms.

One day, in Italian fashion, he embraced the poor man with affectionate warmth. This was the turning-point. The little mark of friendship had won his heart. There was no longer any necessity to seek him out. He haunted Gerard like his shadow. At last the Saint saw that the hour had come for action.

Having brought his captive of love into the Community Oratory, he knelt down before him, and then with tears in his eyes, made an appeal to his better feelings and higher nature.

"My dear friend," he said, "I cannot understand how you are able to live at enmity with God and yet always be so cheerful. You cannot deny that you are a married man, and that your wife is living in Rome. How, then, is it that you venture to pretend to be unmarried? How can you bring yourself thus to play a poor woman false?"

The Saint continued in this strain, until at last, utterly overcome, the unhappy wretch knelt down in his turn, acknowledged everything, and entreated Saint Gerard to pray for him, and tell him what he should do to recover the friendship of God. Great was the charity with which Gerard now dwelt on the Infinite Mercies of Our Lord, and His welcome for the repentant sinner. He advised the secretary to make his confession at once to Father Fiocchi, who happened to be in the House. His confession over, he went to the church to prepare for Holy Communion, when a new prodigy occurred – Gerard went up to him, and asked him where he was going.

"To Holy Communion!" was the reply, given with some eagerness.

"Wait," said Gerard, "you forgot such and such a sin. Go to confession again, and then you will have nothing on your conscience when Our Lord comes to visit you."

Utterly amazed, the secretary went back to confess the sin which he had completely forgotten until thus miraculously reminded, and then, his soul refreshed by a second Absolution, full of joy he received the Bread of Life.

This conversion was both sincere and lasting. No one could help observing the change that had come over the demeanour of the once jovial secretary, until the Archbishop himself asked him the cause. In the fervour of his repentance, Gerard's convert did not hesitate to acknowledge all, and ended with the words of the Samaritan woman in the Gospel:

"Come and see the man who has told me everything that I have done."

Full of surprise, the Archbishop sought Gerard out, and had several long conversations with him. On his departure he earnestly recommended himself to the holy Brother's prayers.

"O my Lord!" replied the Servant of God, "I have need of all the Divine Mercy to save my own soul. I beg of your Grace not to forget me at the Altar."

The Archbishop never lost the impression made upon him during that stay at Caposele.

On their return to the Archiepiscopal Residence, the change in the secretary was the common talk of the place. All his former gaiety seemed to have suddenly disappeared. One day the

Superior of the seminary asked him whatever could have happened to him during his absence.

Then he too was told the wonderful story. The poor secretary made no secret of the fact that he could never again be lighthearted as of old until he had made reparation to his injured wife. As soon as the necessary arrangements could be made, he left for Rome to rejoin the woman whom he had treated so badly, and who thus recovered both her happiness and her husband through the instrumentality of Saint Gerard.

Even in Rome the story was spread far and wide, and at last a Cardinal wrote to ask that the wonderful Brother should be sent to the Eternal City. But when this letter reached Caposele, alas! Gerard was already dead.

HIS LAST JOURNEY

New buildings were at this time in course of erection at Caposele, and immediately after his second return from Naples, Saint Gerard was appointed clerk of the works.

At first sight it might have been thought that the extremely delicate state of his health, and his marked attraction for the contemplative life, would have rendered him unsuited for this occupation. His Superiors, however, knew well that – as the Apostle reminds us – genuine "piety is useful for all things;" (I Timothy 4:8) while Gerard, on his side, in the true spirit of his vocation, had long since learned to unite the activity of Martha with the repose of Mary, and never hesitated to leave his Master's feet to do his Master's work. He was, as usual, indefatigable in his new office. Ever at the post of duty, he did not know what it was to spare himself. He saw to everything, provided for everything, was to be found everywhere. While Gerard was superintending the progress of the building, nothing could fail, for God was with him.

One day the Rector told him that he had come

to the end of his resources. He had no more money with which to pay the workmen.

"Write a letter, Reverend Father, to Our Lord in the Blessed Sacrament," was the holy Brother's suggestion.

The letter was written, and Gerard himself was commissioned to lay it before the Throne of Grace and Mercy. Accordingly he hastened into the church, the petition in his hand, placed it upon the Altar, and then with a familiarity, in which love for once triumphed over reverence, ventured to knock softly at the door of the Tabernacle and say:

"Behold, O Lord, our prayer! Now it is for Thee to answer!"

On Saturday the wages had to be paid. The whole of the preceding Friday night Saint Gerard spent in the church, imploring Our Lord to come to his aid, and to that of the Community. His confidence did not fail of its reward. At break of day he knocked a second time at the Tabernacle door, entreating the Divine Prisoner of Love not to forget his children's needs. He had not yet come down the steps of the Sanctuary, before he heard a ring at the convent door. Hastening to the hall, he found there two bags full of money, which he took with much thankfulness to the Rector. Once more, all that the Superior could find to say was, that Gerard was the spoiled child of Divine Providence.

However, it was clearly not right to tempt Almighty God by neglecting the step required by common prudence. Unless the buildings' were to be left in an altogether unfinished condition it was necessary that money should be raised without further delay.

Therefore, after the Archbishop had granted the necessary permission, it was determined to send two of the Lay-brothers on a "questing" expedition through the diocese.

The Father Rector straightway thought of Saint Gerard as the most suitable person that he could hope to find for this delicate office. But the Saint's health was so shattered, and the heat of the Italian dog-days threatened to be so excessive, that his Superior hesitated. However, he sent for the holy Brother and asked him how he would be able to bear the fatigue of the proposed journey. There was no delay about the answer; he was ready, he said, for anything. Still the Father Director was not satisfied. Laying his hand on Gerard's head, without speaking a word, in his own mind he formed the sentence:

"In the Name of the Most Holy Trinity, I wish that you should be well, and that you should go and make this quest."

Gerard looked at the Rector and smiled. On being asked at what he was laughing, he replied:

"Your Reverence speaks, and yet you do not speak. You wish me to be well and to make this quest – I will be well and I will make the quest. Yes, O Lord, I wish to be well. I wish to obey."

Thus he started, obedience on his lips, obedience in his heart.

From the very commencement miracles cast a halo round his path. The first village in which he made an appearance was called Senerchia. Here they were just on the point of completing the construction of a new parish church. The villagers were in great trouble about some large chestnut-trees that were required as timber for the roof.

They had been duly felled, but no effort could drag them down from the neighbouring mountain, where they were lying uselessly on the ground.

"Take courage," cried Gerard, when he heard of this difficulty, "the church belongs to God, and God will see that it is finished. Let us go to the mountain."

On his arrival the Saint knelt down to beg the blessing of Heaven. Then attaching his handkerchief to one of the largest of the trees, which was so heavy that neither oxen nor buffaloes had been able to move it, he cried out:

"In the name of the Most Holy Trinity, O creature of God, I order thee to follow me."

Then, to the amazement of all the spectators, he dragged it, alone and without effort, down to the valley. The rest of the trees were likewise without further obstacles successfully brought to the church.

Other marvels followed fast. A poor mother was dying in pains of childbirth. Saint Gerard's help was implored in her behalf. He prayed for her and saved her life. This is the first time that he is recorded to have assisted a woman in such a necessity, but since his holy death, again and again has his intercession been asked that some mother might be preserved from imminent danger, and her child be safely brought to the cleansing waters of Baptism. Numerous votive offerings around his shrine attest that his aid has not been sought in vain. "Some Saints can help us in one trouble, others in another," writes Saint Teresa in a well-known passage. This seems to be Saint Gerard's special prerogative in Heaven – to help women, about to become mothers, who are recommended to his kindly care, and to bring them safely through their dreaded travail.

A few days after his arrival at Senerchia, when praying in the old church of the place, he was suddenly raised from the ground, as though by an invisible force, and remained for some time suspended in mid-air without support. The story was carried into the village by those in the church, and a number of people hastened to see him in this miraculous state. Henceforward the whole parish venerated him as a Saint. This veneration greatly increased after his death.

Evidence was given, in the cause of his canonization, that all the inhabitants of Senerchia had chosen Saint Gerard as their special Patron, and that it was the custom of everyone in the place to add a Pater, Ave, and Gloria to their ordinary morning prayers in order to thank the Most Holy Trinity for all the wonderful gifts and graces bestowed on this great Servant of God.

From Senerchia Gerard wrote to the Archpriest of Oliveto, Don Angelo Salvatore by name, to give him due notice of his intended visit.

"Your Reverence has long wished to make the acquaintance of the sinner who is writing to you, and now your wishes will be gratified." Thus did he finish his letter.

These words greatly astonished the Priest. He had indeed long desired to know one about whom he had heard so much, but this he had never told to any living being.

The Saint's stay at Oliveto was rendered noteworthy by many marvels; of these we can only mention one. On the very day of his arrival, as it was dinner-time and Gerard had not yet come

down, his host went to look for him. To his amazement he found his guest in his room, rapt in ecstasy and raised from the ground. He went away,
and returning after some time found the holy
Brother still in the same supernatural condition.
At last Gerard appeared at dinner. He did not
know that he had been seen in ecstasy, and remarked politely that he trusted that his visit might
give no trouble to anyone, but that everything
would go on just as usual, exactly as if he were not
staying in the house at all. Don Salvatore afterwards marked on the wall of the room the exact
height to which he had seen the Servant of God
raised in the air.

From Oliveto Gerard resumed his journey. At a
place called Vietri a woman of abandoned life
came up to him and asked him, as a sort of joke, to
give her a picture of the Blessed Virgin.

"Here is one," was the reply, "but do you look
to the affairs of your soul, and recommend yourself seriously to Our Lady, for you have but a few
days to live."

His words came true. This woman, young and
well when he spoke, was attacked with sudden illness on her return home. Mindful of the warning
of a Saint, she at once sent for a Priest, made her
peace with God, and died in excellent dispositions
three days afterwards.

In the little town of Auletta there was a young
girl who, from her infancy, had been unable to
walk a single step; she had been obliged to lie on
her back all her life, a helpless invalid. When Saint
Gerard saw her, his heart was filled with pity.

"It is nothing," he cried, "the child can walk
perfectly."

Then he called her to him. "Come to me, my child."

That moment she leaped up – she was able to walk as well as anyone in the room. The bystanders cried out in wonderment:

"A miracle! a miracle!"

Covered with a holy confusion, the Servant of God ran away to hide himself. He sought refuge in the house of a Priest, who has left posterity an account of the whole incident. The people, however, pursued him, exclaiming:

"The Saint! where is the Saint?"

Whereupon Gerard made his escape in all haste by a back door, and left the place without further delay.

This cure was radical in its effects. Several years afterwards there was pointed out to a Redemptorist Lay-brother, passing through Auletta, the girl who had been given the use of her limbs by the famous Brother Gerard.

In his humility a fugitive from the applause of men, our Saint next turned his steps to the village of San Gregorio. Here he received hospitality from the Parish Priest, to whom he was personally unknown. But it was impossible for Saint Gerard's light to remain for any length of time hidden under a bushel. The day after his arrival a visitor called at the house. Suddenly, as they were engaged in conversation, Gerard turned abruptly to the Priest with the strange question:

"Reverend Father," he asked, "can you tell me this: If anyone had made up his mind to commit a great sin, and then afterwards, through the grace of God, were to repent and relinquish his criminal design, would that man, I would ask, be still bound to tell his bad intention in confession, even though he never put it into execution?"

The Priest answered the question according to ordinary theological principles, and was much surprised at its apparently motiveless nature. However, a moment after his visitor in stupefaction took him into another room, and said:

"Are you aware, Father, that you have a Saint at present in your house? I am the man of whom he spoke just now. At the instigation of Satan, I was going to commit a certain sin, when suddenly remorse seized me, and I checked myself at the very edge of the abyss. I tell you this to my own confusion and to the glory of your guest."

We now come to the beginning of the end. A severe haemorrhage compelled Gerard to stay his course at San Gregorio. He knew that it was the herald of death. Already at the commencement of the year he had said to Dr. Santorelli, the medical man, who, as we have already seen, was much in his confidence:

"This year I shall die of consumption."

"How can you know that?" asked the doctor.

"I have begged the favour of Our Lord," replied Gerard, "and He has granted it to me."

"But why do you mention consumption rather than anything else?"

"Because that complaint will leave me most to myself," answered the Saint.

A short time before he had told a Lay-brother that he had asked Our Lord to allow him to die of consumption, with no one near him at the end.

This heroic prayer was now about to be granted.

The doctor at San Gregorio did not think

much of the attack, and contented himself with
bleeding his victim. On August 22 Saint Gerard
seemed well enough to leave for the neighbouring
hamlet of Buccino. That same evening a new
haemorrhage came on. Two doctors were hastily
called in, and once more prescribed the universal
panacea of eighteenth-century physicians for all
the ills that flesh is heir to. He was bled anew and
ordered to return without delay to Oliveto, where
the air was thought to be better suited to his pre-
carious state of health. At Oliveto he went to the
hospitable house of his friend, the Archpriest, Don
Salvatore, and thence wrote the following letter to
his Father Rector:

"I wish to inform your Reverence that while
kneeling in the church at San Gregorio, I began to
spit blood. I told a doctor what had occurred. After
examining me, he said several times that this haemorrhage came from the throat, not from the chest,
and assured me that there was no cause for anxiety.
He then bled me, and I seemed to have quite recovered. However, last night at Buccino, as I was
lying down, the same thing happened as at San
Gregorio. Two doctors were summoned at once
and prescribed a second bleeding. . . . They ordered me to return immediately to Oliveto, partly
on account of the climate, and partly that I might
consult the celebrated physician, Don Joseph Salvatore. He is not at present at home, but his
brother, the Archpriest, assures me that he will return this evening. I beg your Reverence to tell me
what to do. Do you wish me to return to Caposele?
If so, I will come back immediately. Should you,
however, desire me to continue the quest, I will
raise no difficulties. My chest really appears to me

to be in a better state than when I left home, and my cough is no worse. Send me a strong Obedience and all will go well. I am very sorry to disturb your Reverence, but do not be alarmed. My dear Father, it is nothing. Recommend me to God, that He may cause me to do His Holy Will in all things."

THE END DRAWS NEAR

The news of Saint Gerard's illness was received with the greatest consternation at Caposele. The Father Rector wrote to him without delay, telling him to remain at Oliveto as long as his kind friends there desired to keep him, and his own health required. He also sent him a companion in the person of a Lay-brother called Francis Fiore.

When this Brother arrived at the Priest's house, he was himself so ill with a violent fever that he could not even mount the stairs to visit our Saint. He had to be put to bed at once on the ground floor. Gerard was then told by the physician, Don Joseph Salvatore, of the illness of the newly arrived Brother Francis.

"Will you have the kindness to tell him from me," said the Servant of God, "that through obedience he must drive away the fever, get up, and come to pay me a visit. Our duties are marked out for us, and I cannot spend my time in nursing a sick man."

The doctor looked amused, and hesitated about delivering such a message. However, as Saint

Gerard insisted, he went downstairs to his second patient. The instant Brother Francis heard what Gerard had said, he rose and went to pay him a visit as he had been told. When the Saint saw him, he said with a gentle smile:

"What a state of things! We have been sent out to make a quest, and you allow yourself to catch a fever! Be obedient, and see that it does not come back again!"

Then, turning to the medical man, he said: "Would you have the kindness just to feel his pulse."

To his utter astonishment, the doctor found that the fever, which had been raging a few minutes before, had now entirely disappeared. Seeing the Archpriest and his brother lost in amazement, Gerard said simply:

"This astounds you. No doubt it looks like a miracle. In reality it is only an effect of obedience."

Either that same day or the next the good physician saw a similar favour granted to his own sister. She, too, was in a high fever. Ill as he was, the Saint managed to go and see her. He simply said:

"There is nothing the matter with you!" As he spoke she was suddenly cured.

A few days previously a shopkeeper of Caposele had been taken very ill. Before having recourse to any human remedies, his son sent to Saint Gerard, begging that he would have the charity to recommend his father to the Blessed Virgin. Gerard replied by a letter. As soon as this letter came to the house the sick man was restored to perfect health.

Seeing and hearing of such marvels as these,

Don Angelo Salvatore determined to endeavour to
obtain from his holy guest a still more remarkable
and important cure. There was living at Oliveto at
the time a Priest named Dominic Sassi, who had
fallen a prey to a strange disease – the consequence
of scruples – which had impaired the use of his
faculties. He remained almost all day shut up in his
room, where he indulged, without any cause, in
terrific yells like those of one distraught. Although
his life had always been irreproachable, he was a
victim to the blackest despair. He only went out at
rare intervals. For seven years he had neither been
able to say Mass nor even to receive any Sacrament. His friends during all this time had not been
idle. They had taken the poor man to the most celebrated places of pilgrimage. All, however, had so
far been without apparent result. God's hour had
not yet come. Here, again, Brother Gerard was to
be the instrument of Our Lord's goodness. When
the Saint was first told of the sad state of this poor
Priest his humility at once took alarm.

"What can I do?" he asked a little coldly.

But soon, as usual, his compassionate chanty
won the day. He went quietly to visit Don Dominic. On beholding the stranger the unfortunate
madman began to send forth his ordinary shrieks.
Gerard was in no way disconcerted. He made the
sign of the Cross upon his head. At once the poor
sufferer grew less violent. Then, seeing a harpsi-
chord in the room, Gerard induced the Priest to
touch it.

The story of David and Saul now repeated itself, but this new David placed the instrument of
soothing in the hands of him to whose soul peace
was once more to come. Together they sang Our

Lady's Litany. At the joyful sound of the sacred music the whole household came running to the room. With grateful hearts all rendered thanks to God. It was evident that the poor Priest was at length completely cured. He might have said Mass the very next morning, but Gerard thought it better for him to be satisfied for the first two days with receiving Holy Communion.

On August 28 he said Mass again, after a lapse of seven years. The whole parish determined to surround the sacred functions with due solemnity. Don Dominic's friends and relations accompanied him to the church. All was ready. Gerard, however, was not present. It was known that he wished to go to Communion at this Mass, so a message was sent to tell him that the Holy Sacrifice was about to commence.

He was found in an ecstasy, the crucifix pressed to his heart, his face pallid as death, his eyes half-closed, insensible to all sounds. The Archpriest, his brother – the physician – and several other persons were summoned. All looked with wonder at the Saint. They left him with God and went quietly away. On their return, after some time, Saint Gerard had come to himself. He suspected that he might have been seen in a supernatural state, so said quietly:

"I slept but little last night. This morning I was overcome by sleep." He then accompanied them to the church.

We may here observe that Don Dominic never again missed Mass. If he ever experienced any difficulty about celebrating the Divine Mysteries it was enough for the Archpriest to tell him to do so in the name of Brother Gerard, and all his trouble

would immediately vanish. When the people heard
the bell ring for his Mass to begin they would always say to one another:

"Let us go and see Brother Gerald's miracle."

Indeed, miracles were heaped on miracles
during these closing weeks of the Saint's life. Thus
one of the Archbishop's brothers went into his
room one day to ask his advice on a matter that
was troubling him, and found the Servant of God
in prayer before a crucifix and raised off the
ground. He thought it better to leave him in peace,
but as he was closing the door Saint Gerard turned
round and spoke to him:

"Don Philip, I know what you have come
about. Have no scruples about such and such matters that are disturbing your conscience. Leave
yourself in the Hands of God's Providence."

These words corresponded exactly to the needs
of Don Philip's soul.

Oliveto heard more than one prophecy at this
time fall from the lips of the Saint. Thus as he was
going away from a certain house he happened to
leave his handkerchief on a chair. A young girl noticed it and handed it to him.

"No," said Saint Gerard, "do you keep it yourself. Perhaps one day it will be of use to you."

As a matter of fact, when, in years to come,
this girl, now married, was in her first confinement,
she was at the point of death. She then invoked her
Holy Patrons, but experienced no relief, until in
her extremity she thought of Brother Gerard's
handkerchief. As soon as this was brought to her
the baby was safely born and all went well. The
witness who has recorded this fact concludes his
statement with the following words:

"My grandmother jealously guarded this Relic. Eventually it came into my possession, but there now only remains in my hands a tiny shred, for I have been obliged, in order to satisfy the devotion of the Faithful, to cut it up into little bits for distribution."

After eight days had been thus spent, full of marvels, at Oliveto, Saint Gerard thought it right to go back to Caposele. He grew daily worse rather than better, and it was quite evident that it would be impossible for him to continue the quest for which he had been sent out of his convent. Under these circumstances, the Archpriest and his brothers could not interpose any obstacles in the way of his return, and all was arranged for his departure. Before leaving Oliveto, never to see it again in this world, the Saint went to say farewell to the family of Don Angelo Pirofalo, whom he held in high esteem. His last words to these friends were in themselves miraculous, and spoke of his approaching death.

"Look sometimes," he said to them, "towards the convent at Caposele. As long as you see a white cloth floating from a window there, so long you will know that I am still alive. When it disappears, you will know that I am dead."

We should remark that Caposele is more than ten miles from Oliveto, and thus it would be, naturally speaking, quite impossible such a distance to distinguish the convent windows. Notwithstanding, Saint Gerard's prediction was fulfilled to the letter. During the rest of his life the mysterious signal was clearly visible at Oliveto. It vanished only at his death.

HIS LAST ILLNESS

On reaching Caposele, Saint Gerard went straight to bed. He was indeed very ill. Reduced to a skeleton, he already looked the picture of death. The haemorrhage was almost continual, and a complication of maladies caused him much pain. In the midst of his sufferings he lost none of his customary tranquillity of spirit. To suffer together with Jesus, under the eyes of His Blessed Mother Mary, had been the longing of his whole life. So now his one request was that a large crucifix and a picture of Our Lady should be placed by his bedside. His gaze was ever on the figure of his Crucified Lord, and from time to time he broke forth into loving exclamations:

"O my Jesus, I suffer much, but it is for Thee Who art dead upon the Cross for love of me. It costs little to suffer, when one suffers for Thee"; or again, "My Jesus, Thou didst die for me. I wish to die to please Thee."

One day the Father Rector found him, as it seemed, in his last agony. All the colour had left his face. His pallor was like that of one from whom life has already departed. Suddenly his eyes fell upon the crucifix. He at once seemed as a man transformed, his face kindled; his cheeks were flushed anew as though in health. The Rector asked in astonishment the meaning of this sudden change. Gerard sighed, and simply said with much animation:

"O Father, great is my longing to be united to my God!"

On the door of his room the Saint had written in large characters, so that they might be ever before him, the words:

"Here is done that which God wills, as God wills, and for as long as He wills it."

His devotion to the Holy Will of God seemed to grow in intensity every day. The Father Rector once seeing his great suffering, asked him if he was perfectly conformed in all things to the Divine Will.

"Yes, Father," replied Saint Gerard in all simplicity, "I think that I am conformed to It. I say to myself that my bed represents God's Will for me, and that on my bed I am nailed to the Most Adorable Will of my God. It even seems to me that the Will of God and myself have become One, so closely are we united together."

He made an equally touching remark to his doctor, who had asked him if he wished to live or to die.

"I do not wish to live," answered Gerard, "nor do I wish to die. I only wish that which God wishes. To say the truth, I should wish to die that I might be united with Him; but at the thoughts of death, I am afflicted at the remembrance that as yet I have suffered nothing for the love of Jesus Christ."

The Saint had many visitors from outside the

convent walls to his sick-room. They were nearly all witnesses of marvellous scenes. Thus one of them, Canon Camillus Boggio, wrote a letter, in which he stated that he visited Saint Gerard almost every day, and often found him rapt in ecstasy. The Canon noticed that as soon as ever the Holy Brother came to himself, he turned his heart to God in fervent prayer.

Meanwhile, as Gerard grew visibly worse, it was thought wise to give him the Holy Viaticum. The whole Community was gathered round his bed, and Father Buonamano, in the enforced absence of the Father Rector, brought the Most Blessed Sacrament. At the approach of Him Who was the only love of his heart, Saint Gerard had himself raised in the bed in the most respectful attitude that was possible; then, before his Communion, he burst out into affections of love and confidence towards Our Divine Lord. After Communion he begged to be left alone. The next day he was much worse. To his other ailments was now added a persistent dysentery, which reduced him to a great state of weakness. It was thought that he would hardly pass the night. But a great change was soon to take place.

Father Fiocchi, who was still Saint Gerard's Director, on hearing of his dangerous illness, sent him an Obedience not to lose any more blood, and to recover his health. This note was given to the Saint. He read it, and then placed it on his breast. Shortly afterwards Dr. Santorelli arrived to pay his usual visit. Seeing the paper in the holy Brother's hands, he asked what it was that he was clasping so tenaciously.

"It is," answered Gerard, "a letter from Father Fiocchi. He orders me not to spit any more blood."

"And what do you mean to do now?" continued the physician.

By way of reply the Servant of God said to the Infirmarian:

"Brother, will you take away that basin? I shall not need it any more."

Nor did he, but the dysentery still continued.

"What is the use," asked Santorelli, "of the one trouble ceasing if the other is to continue?"

The Saint then remarked that the Obedience which he had received did not extend to the dysentery; whereupon the good doctor hastened for one of the Fathers, who asked Saint Gerard how he could have no scruple at only obeying by halves, since it was clear that Father Fiocchi intended him to recover altogether.

"In that case, Father," said Gerard, "I will obey in everything."

When the medical man came again in the afternoon the Saint told him that he would get up next day. As the doctor could not help smiling at this, he added:

"Yes, tomorrow I shall get up, and, if you like, I am ready to eat something now."

The physician hesitated, fearing lest he might hasten his death. However, on seeing him so confident, he began himself to have some hope. He was a man of strong faith, and had often been the witness of marvels worked by Saint Gerard's power with God. A basket of peaches had just been sent to the sick Brother, and the Infirmarian had placed them on the table.

The doctor looked at them and said:

"If you promise me that you will execute the Obedience that you have received, you may eat one of those peaches."

Gerard took one immediately, and a second, and a third. Santorelli then left him, but not without some anxiety. His apprehensions were groundless. Next day, the Feast of Our Lady's Nativity, the holy Brother got up as he had said that he would, and resumed his usual place in the Community. When he appeared once more at dinner in the Refectory the inspired saying of the Wise Man must surely have been in the mind of everyone who saw him:

"The obedient man shall speak of victories."

This is a Divine Promise, and perhaps never before had the words been verified more wondrously than in this recovery of Saint Gerard from the very brink of the grave. But the Saint well knew that it was only for a few short weeks that the time of his pilgrimage was to be prolonged. When one of the Brothers expressed to him the joy of all at seeing his health apparently re-established, he replied at once that God had so disposed it for His Own greater Glory, and in order to show the value of Obedience in His sight, but that in a short while he would be in Eternity. All through the month of September he was getting weaker and weaker. When October came, he was like a ghost in appearance, and evidently could not hold out much longer. On the fourth day of the month he met his friend the doctor, and told him that he had fulfilled the Obedience which had been given him; but that he knew that his end was approaching fast, and that his case was hopeless. The next morning he was forced once more to take to the bed from which he was never more to rise.

Meanwhile, during his short period of convalescence, he had been supernaturally acquainted with the happy death of Sister Mary Celestine Costarosa. It was to this Nun that the first vision concerning the foundation of the Congregation of the Most Holy Redeemer had been vouchsafed by God. Her friendship with Saint Gerard was of old standing, and now her entry into the heavenly country was made known to him from on high. It was the 14th of September, and one of the Lay-brothers, Stephen Sperduto by name, noticing that there was something unwonted about his look that day, asked him the reason.

"Know, my dear brother," answered Gerard, "that this very day at Foggia, the beautiful soul of Sister Mary Celestine has winged its flight to Paradise. She has gone to receive the reward due to her great love for Jesus and Mary."

Soon afterwards the news arrived that the holy Sister, whose name must ever be linked with that of Saint Alphonsus in the Annals of the Congregation, had in truth departed this life at the very time indicated by Saint Gerard.

Another revelation of a similar nature followed shortly afterwards. A painter living at Oliveto, a relation of Don Salvatore, had to go to Caposele on business. Before leaving home he went to see the Archpriest, to find out whether he had any commissions for the convent. The next day he arrived at Caposele early in the morning. Gerard opened the door for him, and said at once:

"The Archpriest is plunged in grief, for his father has just breathed his last."

"It is not possible," replied the painter; "I saw the old man in his son's house last night. He was then in excellent health, and desired to be kindly remembered to you all."

The Saint insisted that he was just dead from a stroke of apoplexy.

"In that case," said the painter, "I must go home to pay him the last respects by being present at his funeral."

"Yes, go at once," answered Gerard, "and tell the Archpriest that he may be quite happy about his excellent father. He has saved his soul."

Thus were the secrets of the other world opened to the gaze of the faithful servant, who was himself so soon to enter the golden portals of the City of his King.

THE DEATH-BED OF A SAINT

The last ten days of Saint Gerard's life, stretched on a bed of intense pain, were days of great suffering, but of perfect conformity to the Divine Will. They were spent in unbroken communion with God. When at last his weakness made vocal prayer difficult, he begged the Lay-brother who was with him as Infirmarian to suggest Acts of resignation, of love, and, above all, of contrition, that he might at least follow them in his heart. This Brother one day asked him if he had any scruples or temptations now that the end was so near. Gerard replied without hesitation that he had through life ever kept Our Lord in view in all his actions. He said that he had had no other desire than to do God's Will in everything, and that therefore he now died in peace and free from anxiety.

On October 12, three days before his happy death, he was suddenly wrapt in ecstasy, and heard to cry out with great joy:

"I see our blessed Father Latessa entering Heaven!"

Father Latessa, we may here state, had died only eight days before. This was the last time that

the secrets of Paradise were unveiled for Gerard's
eyes this side the grave.

The day after this vision was rendered noteworthy by a most consoling favour. A distinguished
ecclesiastic had come to see him, together with his
old friend, Don Joseph Salvatore, the physician
from Oliveto. They brought with them a young
peasant, to whom they had promised that he
should see a great Servant of God. When they arrived at the convent, all three went upstairs to the
sick-room. Notwithstanding his curiosity, the young
villager did not venture to go in, but stood shyly at
the door, where Gerard could not possibly see him.

The holy Brother knew, however, at once that a
stranger was there, and had him called inside. Astonished at hearing himself summoned by name,
the lad went in and glanced, at first with a certain
timidity, at one whom he had heard described as a
Saint. Then he grew bolder and cast his eyes round
the room. They soon fell upon a harp which
chanced to be there. He had never seen anything
of the kind before, and was evidently puzzled at
the meaning of the object. Saint Gerard noticed
his surprise with much amusement, and asked him
to play them something. Everyone laughed at this
proposition, but Gerard insisted. At last he induced
the boy to place his ringers on the instrument,
when lo! sounds of the most ravishing music were
heard at once. Asked how he could thus play un-
taught, the young countryman owned that whilst
he touched the harp his fingers seemed to obey
some irresistible direction.

Surely we may well believe that it was an Angelic visitant who enabled our Saint thus to receive
a foretaste of the celestial harmonies.

The harp which had given forth these heavenly strains to gladden Saint Gerard's gentle spirit, lingering yet on the shores of earth, was carefully preserved in the family of the Santorellis, who had loved him so well and so faithfully.

Two days later, on the Feast of his great Patroness Saint Teresa, Gerard was to give up his soul to God. That morning very early he received a visit from his faithful medical attendant.

"My dear doctor," he said, on seeing him, "mind you recommend me today with all your heart to Saint Teresa, and go to Holy Communion for me."

That he might keep a souvenir of this his last Communion before his eyes even to the end, after he had again received the Holy Viaticum, he asked for the Corporal on which the Blessed Sacrament had just rested, and placed it on his heart, where it remained until all was over. He then plainly stated that he would die before midnight.

"Today," he said, "you are having a recreation day in honour of Saint Teresa. Tomorrow you will have another."

To understand this prediction we must know that the Feast of Saint Teresa is one of the recreation days assigned to Redemptorist Communities by their Rule, while Saint Alphonsus wished that the day after a death should also be always observed as a day of recreation in the house where it occurred. The Holy Founder tells us that though we must naturally grieve for the loss of the Brothers whom we have loved during the years of our Religious Life, still we should rejoice supernaturally at the thought that they have fought the good fight, and that, their labours past, they have now gained "the beautiful crown," which, to quote his own words, he assures us that "Jesus has prepared for those who live in observance and die in the Congregation."

Saint Gerard, then, knew well that the next day the Community would be rejoicing in the Lord at his happy passage to Him, "Whom, not having seen, he had ever loved, in Whom always, though he had seen Him not, he had believed, that he might rejoice with joy unspeakable and glorified, receiving the end of his faith even the salvation of his soul." (I Peter 1:8,9)

"Help me to put on my Habit, Brother," he said to the Infirmarian who was attending him, "for I shall die tonight. I wish to say the Office of the Dead for my own soul."

As the solemn hour drew near when he was to appear before the dread Tribunal of Eternal Justice, his humility was more and more clearly marked. He was ever repeating the most heart-felt Acts of Contrition, in accents of tenderest love that brought tears to the eyes of all who heard him. Shortly before the end, he raised himself up and repeated the Miserere, after each verse repeating the touching words of the royal penitent: "Against Thee only have I sinned, and done evil before Thee. Do Thou cleanse me from my sin."

Thus do the Saints prepare for the first sight of Jesus Christ their Sovereign Judge.

The exact moment of his departure had been revealed to him. In the evening he asked the time. On being told that it was six o'clock, he said that he had just six hours more to live. At this moment the doctor came into the room. Notwithstanding his patient's great weakness, Santorelli did not think the end so near, and even fancied that he seemed a little better than he had been in the morning. As he was leaving, Gerard, contrary to his usual custom, asked him to remain; but as he said that he had other sick people to visit the Saint did not press him further. Next day the good doctor was much distressed. He understood then, when it was too late, that the wonderful Brother had wished him to be present at his last moments.

Towards seven o'clock a messenger arrived from Oliveto. The Archpriest was in difficulty about a chapel that was being built in his parish in honour of Our Lady of Consolation. There was something the matter with the limekiln. He wrote to ask Gerard's prayer that all might go well. The Father Minister read the letter in Gerard's presence. Before he said a word as to its contents, the Saint said quietly:

"Tell the Archpriest to shake some of the dust from the tomb of Saint Teresa, which I will send him, over the limekiln. The accident that he anticipates will then be warded off."

The Archpriest did as was advised by Saint Gerard, and Our Lady's chapel was built without any further mishap.

No one seeing the keenness of perception, and perfect possession of all his faculties which he still enjoyed, would have imagined the agony to be so near. About eight o'clock he seemed momentarily disturbed, and said several times very earnestly:

"O my God, where art Thou? O my Lord, show Thyself to me!"

The Brother who was with him asked him if there was anything that disturbed his conscience.

"Why do you speak to me of disturbance of conscience?" he replied quickly.

Shortly afterwards this same Brother said to him:

"My dear Brother, we have always loved one another. Will you remember me in the presence of God?"

"How could I ever forget you?" answered Gerard.

Between ten and eleven o'clock he fainted away. On coming to himself he appeared very much agitated, and cried out:

"Quick! Brother, quick! Drive away those wretched creatures – what are they doing here?"

The Brother could only conjecture that they were evil spirits allowed, for his greater merit, to make their last fruitless onslaught on the dying Servant of God. The trouble, whatever it may have been, lasted but a few moments. Very soon his countenance regained its wonted calm, and, suddenly kneeling on his bed, he exclaimed:

"Behold the Madonna! Let us pay her homage."

Our Lady had doubtless willed, in her loving kindness, to give her faithful child a foretaste of heavenly bliss. She, the beauteous Dawn, that ever heralds the rising of the Sun of Justice, would thus gladden that chamber, dark with death, by the brightness of her coming before the breaking of the perfect day. It was the answer to a life-long prayer. Jesus had visited him that morning in the Most Holy Viaticum, and now his Mother Mary was by his side. Death was not death for Brother Gerard. It was rather a sweet repose, a falling to sleep on the Sacred Heart of Jesus, beneath the smile of the gentle Virgin Mother. As we think of such an end to life's hard battle as this of Gerard, the aspiration rises almost involuntarily to our lips, that we may learn with him so to love Jesus and Mary here below, that in our time of greatest need, Jesus and Mary may be with us as They were of old with Their servant Gerard.

About half an hour before midnight he asked for something to cool his throat. The Infirmarian went for some water, but as the refectory door was locked he was away for some little time. On his return he found the Saint facing towards the wall, and thought that he was sleeping. A few minutes afterwards he saw him turn round and heard him give a deep sigh. Then he knew that the last agony had already commenced. The Father Minister was summoned at once, and arrived just in time to give Absolution to the holy Brother as his soul was passing away to God Who made it.

The Community, reassured by the doctor, had gone to rest as usual after night prayers. Thus was fulfilled Saint Gerard's earnest prayer that he might be conformed to the Image of his Lord even to the end, and might pass away almost alone, uncomforted by any words of human consolation.

He was in the thirtieth year of his age, and the seventh of his Religious Life, having been professed only a little more than three years.

It was on the feast of Saint Teresa, in the year 1756, that Gerard died. His feast is now kept on October 16, the day after the anniversary of his happy and glorious death.

GLORIFIED IN HEAVEN AND ON EARTH

G erard had scarcely breathed his last when he appeared to a lady who had held him in great veneration during his life. He was, on the occasion of this first apparition after death, still clothed in his Religious Habit, but shortly afterwards he was seen by her again, now resplendent with the Light of everlasting glory.

"Oh," he said, "how liberally does God reward the small sufferings that we endure for His sake on earth!"

He also appeared at the same time in another place to a Redemptorist Father named Peter Petrella, to whom he revealed some of the happiness which he enjoyed in Heaven.

About three hours after the death of this great Servant of God, the Superior of the house, moved no doubt by a Divine impulse, determined to ask of God a supernatural sign of his sanctity. Taking his right arm, he said aloud:

"Gerard, you were ever obedient during life, I now command you in the Name of the Most Holy Trinity, and in that of the Blessed Mother of God, to give us the proof we ask."

He then made an incision in one of his veins, and at once there gushed forth a copious flow of ruby blood. The members of the Community, full of joy, hastened to collect it in a basin, in which they plunged linen cloths, afterwards to be distributed as precious Relics to the favoured friends of the glorious Brother.

When at break of day the sacristan went to announce the death to the neighbourhood, instead of tolling a funeral peal, he rang forth a joyous chime. On being blamed for this, he stated that he had been forced thus to act by an interior impulse that had overcome him when his hand was on the bell-rope. People came flocking in from all sides, as the news of Brother Gerard's departure from this world spread through the country round.

Early in the morning his body had been carried to the church, and it was at once surrounded by an eager throng of persons drawn from all classes of society. In their anxiety to obtain some memorial of the Saint, they began to cut off pieces of his habit, and even of his hair, until it became necessary to set guards to restrain the enthusiasm of the faithful. During the two days that Saint Gerard's remains were in the church, the pious visitors were reckoned not by hundreds but by thousands. There was a constant flow to and from the catafalque of those who had come – many of them from great distances – to do honour to the humble Lay-brother whom God had been pleased to 'raise to such a pinnacle of sanctity.

The funeral took place on October 17. Before finally consigning the body to the tomb, the Superior of the house again opened a vein, and again there gushed forth the red blood that spoke of life rather than of death. Gerard was indeed living still, living and reigning before the Throne of God in Heaven, and men should thus be reminded by stupendous miracles that even the earthly casket of his pure spirit was one day, through the transforming power of the Life-giving Flesh of Jesus Christ, to share in the fulness of the bliss unspeakable that had already been given to his soul, and should be his for endless ages.

On the very day of the interment, the Superior, foreseeing that Gerard would one day be venerated upon our altars, caused a public notary to draw up a formal document embodying the wonders that had taken place between his death and funeral. Besides the Fathers and ten Lay-brothers of the Community, ten of the inhabitants of Caposele were called to give evidence.

All gave their testimony on oath, and the notary made a report, which is to be found in the Process of his Beatification.

Gerard had hardly passed away before it pleased Almighty God to give signs of his power in Heaven. Father Petrella, to whom it will be remembered that the Saint had appeared shortly after his death, was one day asked to pray in an especial manner for a great sinner living at Caposele. He answered:

"I will give Brother Gerard an Obedience to go and find him out and make him enter into himself."

The next day this poor man came in a state of great terror to the convent, saying that Brother Gerard had appeared to him and spoken to him with great severity. He then went to Confession with signs of the most sincere repentance.

A Redemptorist was once speaking to a certain Marchioness of Granafe about the simplicity of Saint Gerard's religious obedience.

"Tell me no more about him," she cried out, "I see clearly that he was only a holy fool!"

"I pray God," replied the Redemptorist, "that you will never be obliged to have recourse to one whom you call 'a fool.'"

Two months had not passed before this lady was attacked by a dangerous illness, and given up by the doctors. In her extreme need she turned to Brother Gerard, and said:

"If you really are the Saint they say, show it, and I will contribute to the expenses of your Beatification!"

Scarcely had she made the promise, than she was completely cured.

Out of the vast number of miracles that Saint Gerard is related to have worked after his death, we will now select the four regarded by the Holy See as proved beyond all reasonable possibility of doubt, and accepted as such for his Beatification.

Joseph Santorelli, grandson of the doctor who attended the Saint with such loving care during his last illness, had a most dangerous attack of typhoid fever. His death seemed so imminent that his relations had actually made all the arrangements for his funeral. It occurred to them, however, to place on his head a picture of Brother Gerard, when immediately, to the stupefaction of all present, the sick man sat up on his bed, completely cured. The Saint had appeared to him, and said:

"Get up without any fear."

In the year 1849 Teresa Deheneffe received a dangerous cut in her left side. For three years the wound got gradually worse. At last the doctors had to perform a very dangerous operation, but it was of no avail. Two days after the operation they pronounced the case to be hopeless. Her Confessor then recommended her to make a Novena to Brother Gerard. At the close of the Novena the bandages and plasters fell off of themselves. The medical men found the sore place healed up, with no trace of any scar, although the evening before it had been a gaping wound, hideous to behold.

The year after this miracle, Ursula Solito was attacked by a frightful cancer, and given up by the doctors, who advised her to receive the Last Sacraments. A picture of the holy Brother was shortly afterwards placed upon her head, and the attendants prayed to him with much fervour. In a few moments she complained that she had received a blow in the front of the cancer, and that she was suffering acute pains. Soon, however, she fell asleep. On awakening she found the doctors round her bed. They examined her with amazement. She was perfectly cured.

"Oh," she said to them, "it is not you who have cured me, it is Brother Gerard!"

In the year 1867 Laurence Riola, a boy ten years of age, was given over by the most distinguished physicians of Naples. The child then begged Brother Gerard to cure him. He fell asleep, and dreamed that he saw a golden ladder resting on his head and reaching up to Heaven. He saw the holy Brother coming down this ladder with a crucifix on his left arm. He touched the child, who at once woke up to find himself quite well again.

Saint Alphonsus, on his bed of death, had pressed to his lips the picture of Saint Gerard. The Holy Founder had wished himself to introduce the cause of the Beatification at Rome. This, however, was, for a variety of reasons, impossible.

It was not until the year 1843 that sixty witnesses were examined on oath at Muro, the place of his birth, and ninety-four at Caposele, where he had died, concerning the virtues and miracles of Brother Gerard Majella. This sworn testimony was sent to Rome, and in the September of 1847, Pope Pius IX, of glorious memory, at the prayer of the King of Naples, of forty-seven Archbishops and Bishops of that Kingdom, and of many other persons of distinction, signed the decree by which his case was formally brought before the Apostolic See.

Thirty years later, in the presence of a large number of Bishops, who had come to the Holy City to celebrate his Episcopal Jubilee, the Sovereign Pontiff solemnly declared that this Venerable Servant of God had practised the Christian Virtues in a heroic degree.

Pius IX went to his everlasting reward the following year. It was reserved for his successor, the great Leo XIII, to inscribe Gerard's name in the white roll of the Beatified.

The sacred ceremony of his solemn Beatification took place with great pomp on Septuagesima Sunday, January 29, 1893, the fifth anniversary of the Beatification of another son of Saint Alphonsus who has since been canonized, Clement Mary Hofbauer.

The following two marvellous cures were recognized as certainly miraculous by the present

Holy Father, Pius X, on the Feast of the Assumption of Our Lady, 1904, in view of the canonization of the wonderful Brother.

In August, 1893, Valeria Baerts of Saint Trond, in the diocese of Liege in Belgium, was dying. She had reached the last stage of some malignant fever, together with meningitis. All the signs of approaching dissolution had already appeared, and the doctors were waiting for the end, which, as they said, was very near. It was in this extremity that Valeria's mother applied a relic of Saint Gerard and begged him to cure her daughter. When the medical men returned to the room they found her in her normal state of health.

In the year 1896 a boy named Vincent de Geronimo, aged fifteen, was studying in the Seminary of Campsano, when he fell ill. The illness increased daily until his danger became extreme. The skill, diligence, and assiduity of the doctors, even of the most skilful, were of no avail in giving him any alleviation: all the symptoms, indeed, showed that death was certain. A relic of Saint Gerard was laid on the breast of the sufferer, when he immediately fell asleep and, wondrous to relate, awoke perfectly cured.

After these two miracles had been, according to the invariable practice of the Holy See, rigorously examined, and approved by the Pope, there was no further obstacle in the way of Gerard's canonization, which was solemnized in Saint Peter's, on December 11, 1903.

"De stercore erigens pauperem, ut collocet eum cum principibus, cum principibus populi sui."

"Raising the poor from the dunghill, to place him with princes, with the princes of his people."

Ever since he has been enrolled in the cata-
logue of the canonized saints, the cultus of Saint
Gerard has spread marvellously throughout the
Catholic world, and he has worked miracle upon
miracle in favour of his clients, conferring both
temporal and spiritual favours of the most extraordinary character upon those who invoke
his aid.

Of these we can only relate one or two of the
more recent that have taken place in our own
country.

In July, 1906, a Miss Mumford, of Aigburth,
near Liverpool, had been a confirmed invalid for
years, suffering from a spinal complaint, and had
to walk on crutches. She prayed earnestly that
Almighty God would grant her, through the intercession of Saint Gerard, that she might be able to
dispense with her artificial supports – for a complete cure she would not ask. She was then blessed
with the relic of Saint Gerard, and was able at
once to walk without crutches, and has never used
them since. Recently she went on a pilgrimage to
Lourdes in thanksgiving to God.

In December, 1907, Mrs. Sullivan, of 75,
Chatterton Street, Liverpool, gave birth to a child.
An hour or two afterwards she was seized with in-
ternal haemorrhage. Two doctors were called in,
and declared the case to be hopeless. The haemorrhage, they said, would certainly return. The
parish priest, Father Jeanrenaud, of the Oratory of
Saint Philip Neri, Maryland Street, was then sent
for. On his arrival the poor woman was in a co-
matose state. He said some prayers to Saint Gerard, and blessed her with the relic. Twice in the
evening he repeated his visit, each time invoking

the Saint, and blessing her with the relic as before. The next morning she was perfectly well. The doctors were amazed, and declared that it was beyond all doubt a miracle. She is now a healthy and strong woman.

One marvel more remains to be related. The ecclesiastical authorities having ordered that all the Relics of the Servant of God should be officially examined, Gerard's tomb was opened for the first time on June 26, 1856. It was then noticed that a mysterious oil oozed forth in such abundance from the brain and bones as to fill up more than one basin. This wonderful Manna – as the Italians call it – was carefully preserved in handkerchiefs and napkins, and was the source of many graces conferred upon the sick who used it with faith, imploring the powerful intercession of God's holy servant, Gerard.

On October 11 the body of the Saint was again examined by ecclesiastical authority, in presence of two doctors. They found the bones more or less damp, but as this could be attributed to the humidity of the soil, it attracted but little attention. They were dried with all due care, and then placed in a chest lined with white silk. Four hours later the chest having been opened, it was discovered that a kind of white oil, shedding a sweet fragrance, was coming forth anew from the holy Relics, and resting like drops of dew upon the silk lining. After a short examination the physicians drew up an official report of this occurrence, which in their opinion was beyond the laws of nature.

"It is needless," writes an eyewitness, "to state how much joy this event has caused us. It is without doubt a presage of the favours which the holy Brother will bestow upon those that honour him."

In the course of one of his characteristic and most beautiful addresses, Pope Pius IX once paid the following testimony to Saint Gerard's sanctity:

"Even as Saint Alphonsus, by his sanctity, zeal, and learning, was a wonderful example for his children, so Gerard by his simplicity of heart and marvellous obedience was a perfect model for those of his own condition – the Lay-brothers. The austerity of his life made him a victim agreeable to God. He sought the Lord with all his heart, and made his dwelling-place in God, even as God dwelt in him."

Thus spoke the Pontiff, signalizing Gerard's virtues rather than his miracles. With these words of the Vicar of Christ, we may well draw our little work to a conclusion.

Gross indeed would be his error who, in considering Saint Gerard's life, should dwell only on the marvels by which it is illumined, without pausing to admire the interior perfection of soul, to which those marvels gave some external testimony. Simplicity of heart, obedience, self-denial, union of the affections and the will with God – these are virtues that we are all called upon to practise in our measure and degree.

It is, however, to those of his own state of life, to men called to that holy Vocation, which Gerard treasured as the very apple of his eye, that he will ever be, in a most special way, a patron and a model. To all Lay-brothers he is a bright example, but particularly to those of his own beloved Congregation. As they go about their daily duties, they may remember that what they do now, he did once. There is no office of a Redemptorist Lay-brother that was not discharged by Saint Gerard Majella. He was at different times, tailor, gardener, cook, refectorian, sacristan, infirmarian, carpenter. He had learned at Naples to make crucifixes, and afterwards employed himself at this work in his leisure moments at Caposele. He was clerk of the works during the progress of the convent buildings. He went on Mission with the Fathers to attend to their wants. All these duties he performed with equal care, knowing that all were the Will of God for him.

Divine Providence has then given him to us as a great Saint, who rejoiced in the careful discharge of humble offices, knowing that nothing is really small that is done with a single eye for the glory of God. The Brothers whom Saint Gerard loves with a deep fraternal love may ever remember to their comfort that their work, of little account in the eyes of men, is that by which he became so great in the eyes of God; while it was his charity – the virtue which all who would save their souls must practice – that made him so dear to the Sacred Heart of Our Lord Jesus Christ, and also to those – his brethren here below – whose lives grew sweet and pleasant through the fragrance of his heavenly and also of his human loving-kindness.

NOTES

SAINT GERARD'S RULE

The following resolutions of Saint Gerard are taken from Chapter 10.

I. O my God and my only Love, today and every day I give myself up to Thy Good Pleasure. In all temptations and trials, I will say always "Thy will be done." All that Thou mayest ordain for me I will embrace with my whole heart, never ceasing to raise my eyes to Heaven, there to adore the Divine Hands which cast towards me the precious pearls of Thy Most Holy Will.

II. Lord Jesus, I wish to carry out all that is commanded me by my Mother the Holy Catholic Church.

III. My Jesus, through love of Thee I will obey my Superiors as Thy Divine Person made visible to my sight. I will live as though I were no longer myself, striving to conform myself to the judgment and will of those who command me, always certain of finding Thee in them.

IV. Amongst all the virtues which are dear to Thee, O my God, that which I love with a love of predilection is holy Purity. My trust is in Thee, O Infinite Holiness, to preserve me from any thought which might sully the brightness of my soul.

V. I will only speak in three cases: when the glory of God is at stake; when the interests of my neighbour may demand it; or when it is necessary for some personal reason.

VI. At recreation I will speak only when I am spoken to, except in one of the three cases mentioned above.

VII. Instead of any words that I might be tempted to speak to the displeasure of God, I will say: "My Jesus, I love Thee with my whole heart."

VIII. I will say nothing either good or bad about myself. I will act as if there were no such person as I in existence.

IX. I will never excuse myself whatever reason I may have for doing so, unless any sin against God would result from my silence, or any harm to my fellowman.

X. I will oppose all that which opposes Regular Observance in the Community.

XI. I will never answer when I am blamed, unless I am told to do so.

XII. I will attack no one in conversation, nor will I make any reference to the faults of my neighbours, even by way of a joke.

XIII. I will be careful to excuse everyone, considering in my neighbour the Person of Jesus Christ Himself, Whom the Jews accused, notwithstanding His innocence. I will defend others, especially in their absence.

XIV. If anyone should speak ill of another, I will warn him of his fault, even though he be the Father General.

XV. I will do my utmost to manage that others should be spared any occasion of annoyance.

XVI. If I should notice anyone committing a fault, I will be careful not to correct him in the presence of others. I will speak to him on the matter between ourselves, and in a low tone of voice.

XVII. As soon as I see a Father or Brother in any need of assistance, I will leave all to help him, if I can do so consistently with obedience.

XVIII. I will visit the sick, always with the necessary permission, several times every day.

XIX. Never will I mix myself up with anyone else's business. I will never say that anyone has done anything badly.

XX. Whenever I am told to help others in their work, I will obey the responsible person exactly and without remark. I will never allow myself to say that anything is not done as it should be. Still, when I know from experience how things should be carried out, I will give my advice, but never in the tone of a master.

XXI. When I am joined with others in discharging the duties of the house, however trivial they may be (sweeping the corridors, moving furniture, and the like), I will make it my rule never to be anxious to get the best place or the best things. Conveniences I will yield to others, taking for myself what God may leave me. Thus everyone will be pleased, myself among the rest.

XXII. I will never put myself forward to discharge any duty, but will wait until I am told what to do.

XXIII. In the Refectory I will not look about, unless obliged to do so by duty or charity

XXIV. I will take from the board at meals the plate that is nearest to me without looking at the others.

XXV. In all my interior conflicts, I will be careful not to listen to self-love. If anyone blames or accuses me, I will strive to make all bitter feelings pass gently away. Then tranquillity will reign at the bottom of my soul.

XXVI. My supreme resolution is to give myself unreservedly to God. For this reason I will endeavour to have continually before my eyes this motto: "Be thou deaf, blind, and mute."

XXVII. I will not know the meaning of the words "I will" or "I will not." Only one thing do I desire – Thy good pleasure, O my God, and not mine own. In me, O Lord, may Thy Will, not mine, be done.

XXVIII. To do the Will of God it is necessary that I should give up mine own. I wish to possess God only; if, then, I wish for God alone, it must needs be that I should detach myself from all that is not God.

XXIX. I will have it at heart to seek my own interests in nothing.

XXX. During all the time of silence, I will meditate within my soul on the Passion and Death of Jesus Christ, and on the Sorrows of Mary.

XXXI. May all my prayers, Communions, and all my good works be always applied for the salvation of poor sinners in union with the Precious Blood of Jesus Christ.

XXXII. If anyone is wanting in the patience necessary for him to endure the trials that God sends him, and ask me to help him, I will pray for his intention, and for three days offer up all that I do in order to obtain for him a perfect conformity with the Divine Will.

XXXIII. When I receive my Superior's Blessing, I will consider that it is Jesus Christ himself from whom I am receiving it.

XXXIV. As a general rule I will not ask permission for Holy Communion overnight. I will only ask it the moment before I am going into the church. Thus I shall always keep myself in readiness. If permission be refused me, I will make a Spiritual Communion, when the Priest communicates sacramentally.

XXXV. My thanksgiving after Communion shall last until midday, and my preparation for next day shall be made from midday until six o'clock in the evening.

XXXVI. In visiting the Blessed Sacrament, I will make the following Acts: "O Lord Jesus, I believe that Thou art present in the Blessed Sacrament, and I adore Thee with all my heart."

"I have the intention of adoring Thee by this visit wherever Thou art present in the Sacred Host, and I offer Thee Thy Precious Blood for poor sinners. Also I desire to receive Thee spiritually as many times as there are sanctuaries on earth in which Thou dost dwell."

XXXVII. I will make these Acts of the Love of God. "O my God, I have the intention of offering Thee as many acts of love as have been ever made Thee by the Most Holy Virgin and all the Saints in Heaven, as well as by all the Faithful on earth. I would love Thee as much as Jesus Christ loves Thee, and as He loved His chosen ones. I would renew these acts with every beating of my heart. I offer these my desires to my Mother Mary."

XXXVIII. I will have all possible veneration for Priests, beholding in them Jesus Christ Himself, and striving to be penetrated with the greatness of their dignity."

BILOCATION

Saint Thomas, the Thomists generally, Vasquez and some other Theologians deny that the same body can, even by miracle, exist circumscriptively in two different places at the same time. They are consequently obliged to account for any cases of Bilocation or Multilocation – if admitted to be real – in one of the three following ways:

1. *Per visionem imaginariam* – i.e., the imagination is impressed (miraculously) with a picture of a Saint not physically present.

2. *Per representationem extrinsecam in aliquo corpore aereo* – i.e., a real external image of the Saint is produced by God and seen by those to whom he appears, though he himself is not there.

3. *Per visionem corporalem qua videtur Sanctus, licet sit longe distans* – i.e., the Saint himself is really seen through all the intervening space, as though he were present.

However, Suarez, De Lugo, and with them the greater number of Theologians hold against Saint Thomas that circumscriptive Multilocation is possible by miracle. They can therefore, if they please, thus account without difficulty for the Bilocation of

Saints during life; but many even of these authors prefer to explain this wonderful fact in one of the modes just mentioned, – as for the most part they explain the Apparitions of Our Lord from Heaven (always excepting the three great Apparitions to His Holy Mother on occasion of her Death and Assumption, to Saint Peter on the Appian Way, and to Saint Paul on the road to Damascus, – cases in which it seems to be almost certain that either Our Lord in His Sacred Humanity left Heaven for the moment, or that there was by miracle a circumscriptive Bilocation of His glorified Body), as well as those of the Blessed Virgin and of the Saints after their death.

Theologians generally discuss these questions when treating of the Eucharist and of the Mysteries of Our Lord's Life. Perhaps the most satisfactory treatment of the whole subject is that to be found in "Suarez De Mysteriis Vitas Christi," Disp. li., sec. 4, and "De Euch.," Disp. xlviii., sec. 4, n. 5 to n. 17.

* * *

This purely spiritual presence seems to be analogous to the purely intellectual vision, which as writers on Mystical Theology – following in the steps of Saint Augustine – tell us is the highest species of vision vouchsafed by Our Lord to His servants here below. Such an experience may be explained without difficulty, as in the case of corporal bilocation, on some hypothesis of sensations miraculously produced by Almighty God – with the obvious difference that the impressions made upon the recipient of these sensations would be made otherwise than through the sense of sight. However, it may perhaps also be accounted for by the replication of the soul alone, or by the enlargement of its sphere of activity. In a sermon on " The Mysteriousness of our Present Being," Dr. Newman speaks as though the limitation of the soul's activity to the body were the wonder that really needs explanation.

"The body," he writes, "is made of matter. This we see; it has a certain extension, make, form, and solidity; by the soul we mean that invisible principle which thinks. Each man is sure that he is distinct from the body, though joined to it, because he is one, and the body is not one, but a collection of many things. He feels, moreover, that he is distinct from it because he uses it, for what a man can use, in that he is superior. No one can by any possibility mistake his body for himself. It is his; it is not he. This principle, then, which thinks and acts in the body, and which each person feels to be himself, we call the soul. Hence we call the soul spiritual and immaterial, and say that it has no parts, and is of no size at all. All this seems undeniable. Yet observe if all this be true, what is meant by saying that it is in the body, any more than by saying that a thought or a hope is in a stone or a tree? How is it joined to the body? What keeps it one with the body? What keeps it in the body? What prevents it any moment from separating from the body? When two things which we see are united, they are united by some connexion which we can understand. A chain or cable keeps a ship in its place; we lay the foundation of a building in the earth, and the building endures. But what is it which unites soul and body? How do they touch? How do they keep together? How is it that we do not wander to the stars or the depths of the sea, or to and fro as chance may carry us, while our body remains where it was on earth? Certainly it is as incomprehensible as anything can be, how soul and body can make up one man; and unless we had the instance before our eyes, we should seem in saying so to be using words without meaning. For instance, would it not be extravagant and idle to speak of time as deep or high, or of space as quick or slow? . . . It is certain, then, that experience outstrips reason in its capacity of knowledge; why, then, should reason circumscribe faith when it cannot compass sight?" – Parochial and Plain Sermons

INVISIBILITY

We read in the life of Blessed Lidwina that two men once commenced quarrelling near her house. One of them fled for safety to the sick-room of the Saint; the other pursued him, sword in hand. Furious with rage, he asked Lidwina's mother if his enemy was not there. She answered "No." He did not believe her, and asked the Saint the same question. Unable to tell what she deemed a lie, Lidwina said "Yes," receiving in punishment a blow on the cheek from her mother. She then said that she trusted in God that He would hide the poor man who had sought safety in her room. As a matter of fact, his wrathful foe was unable to see him, and was forced to go away without having been able to satisfy his thirst for vengeance.

It is told of Saint Lucien in his Acts that when he walked through the streets he was seen by those by whom he wished to be seen, and was invisible to all others.

The King of Naples having sent sixty soldiers to seize Saint Francis De Paula, the Saint prostrated himself in prayer before the High Altar in the church. The soldiers went to the church to find him, passed close to him, and even touched him, but were unable to see him.

Violante, wife of John, King of Aragon, wished out of curiosity to see the interior of Saint Vincent Ferrer's cell. As the Saint refused to comply with her desires, one day she had the door forced in and made her entrance. She then saw everything that the cell contained except its occupant. The same thing happened to her attendants. She then asked the other Dominicans where was Vincent. They answered that he was in her presence, and that they could not understand her not seeing him. Then they asked him, "Why do you not make yourself known to the Queen? She has come to see you. Why then do you not speak to her?"

"I have never yet given permission to any woman to enter my cell," answered the Saint; "not even to the Queen. By a punishment of God her eyes are holden so that she may not see me as long as she remains here." The Queen went out immediately. Saint Vincent followed her. She then asked his pardon for her conduct, and returned home.

www.ingramcontent.com/pod-product-compliance
Lightning Source LLC
Chambersburg PA
CBHW031316120626
46554CB00001BA/427